SUCCESS
IN
BABYLON

JOHN W. STANKO

urbanpress

Success in Babylon
by John W. Stanko
Copyright ©2020, 2023 John W. Stanko

ISBN 978-1-63360-224-3

For Worldwide Distribution
Printed in the U.S.A.

Urban Press
P.O. Box 8881
Pittsburgh, PA 15221-0881
412.646.2780

CONTENTS

ABOUT THE AUTHOR

INTRODUCTION

In case you haven't noticed, the followers of the Lord are no longer in charge in Western culture, and the Church doesn't quite know what to do about it or how to respond. Some respond with anger at the proliferation of decisions and lifestyles that violate biblical standards—although not everyone understands or agrees with what the standards should be. Others have tried to make peace and adopt some of the basic cultural norms like dress, music, and gender roles, but others have circled the wagons, so to speak, to hold down the historical standards until help arrives. Such help would be in the form of a revival or another great awakening that will turn the hearts of the people toward the Lord.

I have heard members of my generation lament the rise of social media and some have refused to participate, sort of like my immigrant grandmother who never had a phone in her house. We had to call the neighbors and they had to go get her if we needed to talk. My grandmother was cute and quaint, but no one wanted to emulate her. As soon as her eleven children got out of her house, they all had phones installed. I just smile and shake my head when I hear some say, "We don't know how to talk to one another. We need to get our noses out of our phones and back to the dinner table or small groups or church." That sounds good and is a noble aspiration, but it will never happen.

If we are not careful and continue to react to

cultural changes, choosing to retreat into our spiritual ghettos where we are safe from the "bad people," we will become what I call cultural Amish. You know the Amish, those people who still drive horse-drawn carriages, grow beards, wear straw hats or doilies on their heads, and don't use electricity or other "modern conveniences." The Amish reside quite close to where I live and I have often gone to visit them to buy their vegetables, visit their farms, and observe their way of life. Many other "tourists" do the same.

Yet I have never heard of anyone who visited the Amish and walked away thinking, "I want to be one of them." No one buys a hat, grows a beard, and says, "I'm converting." Maybe they have and I don't hear about it. My point is that the Amish are model Christians, hard-working, family-oriented people, but the Amish are culturally irrelevant. They have distanced themselves so far from the world that the world does not recognize or relate to who they are. And they are not thought of as Christian but as Amish, a communal culture that has some unique, old-fashioned values. The modern Church risks becoming spiritual Amish when we attempt to withdraw as a strategy to deal with the world and its wicked ways. We are still trying to figure out how to fulfill Jesus' prayer that we would be in but not of the world. We tend to err on either extreme, being totally in or totally out.

I am not smart enough to prescribe what the universal Church's response should be to this trend. All I know is that Christians used to help make the rules, but we no longer have that kind of influence. I am old enough to remember when we started every day in public school with prayer and a Bible reading. I am old enough to remember that people with alternate sexual preferences didn't make them public. I am old enough to remember that there were laws—laws mind you—that forbid certain activities on Sunday, the Sabbath. I am old enough, well, you get the idea chat I am old, and I have had a front row seat to view these changes which have come along with breathtaking speed.

I have heard some declare that we need to pray more. I have visited countries where all-night prayer vigils are attended by thousands. I know other individuals who pray for the reverse of Roe vs. Wade that legalized abortion. I know many who pray for revival and renewal. Some claim we haven't prayed enough and that is why prayer was removed from public schools in the U.S. I have often thought. How do you know that? Is that the cause or was it something else?

In this book, I am going to focus on a man who faced the same dilemma the modern Church faces. Daniel was exiled from his homeland, carried off by the victors after a nasty siege of Jerusalem. Judah had been unfaithful and God had delivered them into the hands of the Babylonians. but it seems that God was up to something else besides punishing the Jews, who had been bad boys and girls. He was breaking down the walls between the world and Judaism, setting the stage for events six centuries later that ushered in the New Covenant through Christ.

God is doing the same thing today as He was in Daniel's day. Some of what the world is experiencing is part of His plan and to resist it is to resist Him. For example, technology and social media are part of His plan. I won't defend that position in this book, but I will say that the Internet is the greatest publishing tool since the printing press. Yet most churches ignore it, only using it if it can undergird and support their face-to-face programs. I maintain that we should be using the Internet to build relationships (yes, it is possible), to disciple believers, and to evangelize.

We are addicted, however, to our face-to-face paradigm and therefore keep waiting for people to return to church, hopefully in droves. What if they don't return? What if the Church needs to update its delivery systems and its expectations of what successful ministry is? What if we need to face that these buildings and some of our programs, both old and new, are increasingly irrelevant in this environment that is increasingly hostile to the Church or for people who are not thinking about "joining" anything, let alone a church. And of course, recent scandals have almost made the word church a bad name. Yet while perverted pedophiles continue to use social media to locate their prey, the church cannot seem to use that same media to woo followers to Jesus.

I first developed some of the material in this book when I was active in prison ministry from 1989-1995 (I told you I was old). I explain in chapter one why I chose Daniel and Babylon as my model for prison ministry but let me quickly emphasize that I was part of a team that conducted these seminars. I did not generate all the material we taught but I have gone beyond what we taught with the subject matter in this book. Please don't think this is a book for inmates. It can certainly help them (and I have addressed a prison audience in each chapter to help them apply what I write in their "world") but it can also help you if you are struggling with modern Babylon and the Church's and your response to it.

My life message that I have delivered all over the world is life purpose, so I attempt to tie much of what is in this book to the concept of finding and fulfilling your purpose in Babylon. In fact, the Church needs to become an expert in helping people find their life purpose as part of our response to Babylon and its increasing influence throughout the world. The title of each chapter in this book is a concept like forgiveness, revelation, influence that ends with the words "in Babylon." The chapters are short and each one ends with questions and tips for how to apply or further consider the points I present.

Please don't misunderstand me. I don't like Babylon and what it stands for. I am concerned for the Church and its future, although I know the gates of hell will not prevail—but that doesn't mean those forces won't try to prevail. The followers of Jesus, usually found in churches, hold the keys to the Kingdom and I want to see us use them as effectively as we once did.

With the convenience of modern travel and communication, there has never been a better time with so many opportunities to serve the Lord. Daniel impacted Babylon but he had to be content with influence and not control and we also have to learn in our modern Babylon how to do the same. The day of the Church controlling the cultural agenda is gone, perhaps forever. At the same time, the day of the Church influencing the cultural agenda has never been greater if we change the way we do "business."

My prayer is that you will define and then find your success in Babylon. If you are in a spiritually-hostile environment at work or in your nation, I want to help you not just survive but thrive. Toward that end, I present for your consideration, *Success in Babylon How to Thrive in a Hostile Spiritual World*.

John W. Stanko
April 2020
Pittsburgh, PA USA

CHAPTER ONE

SUCCESS IN BABYLON

Many years ago, I was part of a team that conducted seminars called *The Lion's Den: God's Most Successful Prisoner* in prisons across the state of Florida. We focused on Daniel and portrayed him as the ideal and model inmate, for he was indeed a prisoner in Babylon—there against his will—yet he prospered in that setting. The inmates loved our seminar, but then we also taught it outside of prison and got the same response. Many people found themselves in a spiritually-hostile environment and could not grasp that God wanted them not just to *survive* there but to *thrive* there. We wanted to help people transition from survive mode to thrive mode.

While in Atlanta recently, a woman prayed for me and said, "I think God is going to show you something new, and He will tell you what it is." Two days later, I was having a casual conversation with other friends when I mentioned *The Lion's Den* as a prison outreach and they immediately said, "You need to write that!" I am not sure if this is the "something new" I was told to be looking for but, in faith, I will assume it is and write about it until God shows me something else that's new.

BABYLON

Let's get started at a good place to start—at the beginning. In Daniel 1:1-2, we read,

In the third year of the reign of Jehoiakim

1

king of Judah, Nebuchadnezzar king of Babylon came to Jerusalem and besieged it. And the Lord delivered Jehoiakim king of Judah into his hand, along with some of the articles from the temple of God. These he carried off to the temple of his god in Babylonia and put in the treasure house of his god.

The Bible has a way of telling us a lot in only a few words. If we are not careful, we don't linger long enough to absorb the details and implications of what we are being told. In those two verses, we learn that:

- Jerusalem was under siege. That means the Babylonians surrounded the city and tried to starve the inhabitants out and into submission, which obviously happened.

- The Babylonians raided and pillaged the Temple, the epitome of Jewish life, worship, and culture. The fall of Jerusalem must have been a traumatic experience involving the death and relocation to Babylon of thousands of people, including Daniel and his family.

- The Babylonians were a religious people with many gods and the king, Nebuchadnezzar, had his own god, for which he had built a temple and a house.

There is much more history that goes with this story, for Nebuchadnezzar had invaded Judah once before, but the Judeans had violated the terms of their peace and surrender, so he came back again, only this time he destroyed what he had originally agreed to preserve. And notice who was behind all these events: "And the Lord delivered Jehoiakim king of Judah into his hand." The Lord was doing something that was bigger than one nation or people group. He was positioning the world to receive their King six centuries later, and this was part of His plan.

THE IMPLICATIONS

In subsequent chapters, we will study what Daniel went through in order to succeed in Babylon because it holds important implications for our day. We are also being asked to serve in Babylon, and we are often not sure how to respond or what to do. Many believers are not comfortable in a foreign or secular setting, so we long for a more spiritually-friendly environment in which we can serve the Lord and others. Yet God has His own plans, just like He did with Daniel in Babylon, and if we can grasp that He is doing the same with us, we can then settle into our situation and serve the Lord. In other words, Babylon as a destination may be a God-assigned place for you.

In our *Lion's Den* seminars, we would tell the inmates that they may be fenced in, but there was no lid or ceiling on their imprisonment. They had no barriers between them and God, and they could pray, worship, and serve vertically while they were limited and imprisoned horizontally. What's more, God had sent them there to learn that important lesson, while He also worked on their character and behavior. The same may be true for you.

Are you in a situation that is neutral or maybe even hostile where God and your faith are concerned? Are you waiting for your circumstances to improve before you express your spiritual gifts and serve those around you? Are you blaming where you are for your lack of spiritual fruit or holiness? If so, you need to learn how to succeed in Babylon, for your Babylon is not going away—and God has no intention of taking you out, at least not right now. What's more, it may be the very mission field God has chosen for you, and your reluctance to accept that reality will hinder your growth and progress.

I urge you to make peace with where you are and set a goal not just to survive where you are but to thrive and prosper there. Over the next few chapters, let's study and learn together what Daniel and his friends did that allowed God to honor them by highlighting their stories for generations to come in His word. Then let's go about establishing our own credentials before God as people who know how to do well in a setting where God seems to be absent, but is very present—at least for you and me who find ourselves in the lion's den.

CHAPTER TWO

CHANGE OF PLANS IN BABYLON

In the last chapter, we looked at the first two verses in the book of Daniel to understand the historical context. In this chapter, let's take a look at the next few verses in Daniel 1:

> Then the king ordered Ashpenaz, chief of his court officials, to bring into the king's service some of the Israelites from the royal family and the nobility young men without any physical defect, handsome, showing aptitude for every kind of learning, well informed, quick to understand, and qualified to serve in the king's palace. He was to teach them the language and literature of the Babylonians. The king assigned them a daily amount of food and wine from the king's table. They were to be trained for three years, and after that they were to enter the king's service. Among those who were chosen were some from Judah: Daniel, Hananiah, Mishael and Azariah. The chief official gave them new names: to Daniel, the name Belteshazzar; to Hananiah, Shadrach; to Mishael, Meshach; and to Azariah, Abednego (Daniel 1:3-7).

I mentioned in the last chapter that I was part

of a team of people that would teach this material about Daniel in Babylon in a prison setting, but we saw that the implications and lessons learned from this story are applicable to any of us, especially if we find ourselves in a culture (business, government, or school) that is neutral or hostile toward God and His values. Let's look at what we can learn from these few verses to help us be successful in our own Babylon.

WHAT DO THESE VERSES TELL US?

In these verses, we learn these young men were:

1. Drafted into service in Babylon; they did not volunteer.

2. The best of their generation, voted most likely to succeed in their high school class (well not really, but they would have been in a modern setting). They were handsome, intelligent, and good students otherwise the king's official would not have chosen them.

3. Forced to attend a Babylonian university and learn a whole new language, currency, culture, and career.

4. Given new names. Every measure was taken to strip them of their previous identity so they could blend into Babylon and serve the king—the same king who had ravaged their land, perhaps killed their families, and forced them to come to Babylon.

5. Placed under the care of the chief of the eunuchs according to one translation. Why would they be placed there unless they had been made eunuchs themselves? Their manhood was altered, through

no fault or choice of their own, and at a young age they found themselves far away from home, serving a pagan king, with all their own plans for the future radically altered or eliminated.

DANIEL'S RESPONSE

After all that happened to him, Daniel made a startling decision as described in Daniel 1:8: "But Daniel resolved not to defile himself with the royal food and wine, and he asked the chief official for permission not to defile himself this way." After all he had been through, Daniel's main concern was still first and foremost serving the Lord and being true to His people's way of life. If I was a teenager or young adult and had been through what Daniel had, the last thing I would have been concerned with was maintaining a kosher lifestyle. I would have been angry, mourning what I had lost.

Yet Daniel was not mourning or miserable; he was focused on being true to who he was and determined not to defile himself. That commitment is admirable, but certainly reveals the reason Daniel distinguished himself from all the others, Even though hundreds of miles from home, even though his whole life and future had been drastically altered, Daniel was a man of principle and refused to surrender to the force of the prevailing culture or the bitterness of resentment. Daniel's behavior was not affected by or related to his environment; he was true to his values and his God. He was determined not to waiver from his trust in God, no matter what he encountered.

What about you? Is your resolve equal to that of Daniel? For it to be so, here are some suggestions. First, make peace with your past and present if today you are not doing what you had envisioned yourself doing earlier in life, or doing it where you had never intended to be. Like Daniel, you may be in your own Babylon, far from the place of your choosing. For me, that place not-of-my-choice is church work, for I was headed to Harvard and a career in business—but God had other plans. I did not go looking for church work but it came looking for me. Resolve that you are in the right place because it is God's place for you, if not your chosen place.

Second, commit yourself to excellence, both in character and work, no matter where you are and what you are doing. Even if you are surrounded by those who do not share your values, be true to what you know the Lord has taught you and strive to produce good work from a willing heart. Finally, deal with any bitterness toward those who have mistreated you or abandoned you in your day of trouble, no matter how recent or long ago they did so.

We will see throughout this book how well Daniel served those who had mistreated and oppressed him, and God wants you to do the same. You cannot serve those whom you hate or resent. Also, make sure you are right with God and don't hold anything against Him because you had to make a change of plans concerning your life and where it would be expressed. If you will take this advice, you will be well on your way to laying the foundation for a successful stay in Babylon, whether for a season or for a lifetime.

CHAPTER THREE
VALUES IN BABYLON

In case you have forgotten since you read it in Chapter one, we are examining how you can survive in a spiritually-hostile environment just like Daniel and his friends did. This is important because modern societies, at least in the West, are becoming increasingly antagonistic to believers and their values, yet Jesus prayed,

> "My prayer is not that you take them out of the world but that you protect them from the evil one. They are not of the world, even as I am not of it. Sanctify them by the truth; your word is truth. As you sent me into the world, I have sent them into the world. For them I sanctify myself, that they too may be truly sanctified" (John 17:15-19).

God is not interested in removing His saints from the world, but wants them to thrive and prosper there, providing a witness for Him to all those who will pay attention. In a sense, Daniel was one of the first missionaries in history, sent to another culture where God expected him to serve and represent Him and His ways. The same may be true for you, so let's look at another lesson we can all learn from Daniel's sojourn in Babylon.

TRUE TO HIS VALUES

We learned in the last chapter that Daniel was subjected to a total makeover in Babylon that included a new name, education, and identity as a man. His family was probably dead, and he found himself far away from his homeland. Any plans of marriage were out of the question. Keep in mind that Daniel was undoubtedly a teenager while all this was going on. If I had been in Daniel's situation, I would have been tempted to abandon my people's values after all I had been through, but that was not who Daniel was. We read,

> But Daniel resolved not to defile himself with the royal food and wine, and he asked the chief official for permission not to defile himself this way. Now God had caused the official to show favor and compassion to Daniel, but the official told Daniel, "I am afraid of my lord the king, who has assigned your food and drink. Why should he see you looking worse than the other young men your age? The king would then have my head because of you" (Daniel 1:8-10).

What can we learn from those verses?

1. Daniel did not rebel against or react to his situation but kept a good attitude. He did not refuse to eat the king's food, he asked permission not to do so. We can speculate what would have happened if his caretaker had refused his request, but the good news is that he did not. He instead gave Daniel permission to abstain.

2. God was intimately involved with Daniel in Babylon. Note that He gave Daniel favor with his guard. That means that God was up to something according to His own purposes in Daniel's life, and He often is doing the same in yours.

3. Daniel's supervisor feared the king: Daniel feared God.

4. The chief feared what would happen if Daniel did not eat the king's food; Daniel was concerned what would happen if he

did. Yet Daniel realized what the guard was after and helped him obtain it, which was healthy recruits who could serve in the king's court.

5. Daniel cooperated with the king's plan and the supervisor's objective, but he had a better way to achieve the same purpose.

Daniel did not boycott the king's food; he did not go on a hunger strike. He did not withhold the best of who he was from people who had misused and abused him. Daniel had confidence that if he obeyed God, then God would work on his behalf and God's role would benefit all involved: Daniel, his friends, the supervisor, and the pagan king. Daniel stayed true to his values and God stayed true to him, and this set Daniel on a path that would lead to promotion and success in Babylon

LESSONS TO APPLY

It has been said that your character is revealed when you are alone and no one is forcing you to do anything, so you are free to respond according to what's in your heart. Daniel's values were deeply embedded in his character, and he stayed true to them, even when he was suffering and under pressure. Can the same be said of you? Tribulation reveals character, and Daniel could have easily assimilated into Babylonian culture, but he did not cross the line into disobedience to the Lord.

Do you live two lives, one a church life and one a non-church life, or do you have and follow the same values in both worlds? Do you count on God's favor in your own Babylon? Do you even recognize His favor, thanking Him for it, and take advantage of it in a good sense? Is your attitude godly, even when you are mistreated or misunderstood? If you are going to succeed in your Babylon, you must take Daniel's example seriously and look to model your own life after his. If you do, God can use and even promote you in Babylon. If you don't, you may survive but you won't thrive, and your days will be much more difficult than they should be if you cooperated and lived life God's way.

CHAPTER FOUR

GOD'S WAYS WORK
IN BABYLON

In the previous chapter, we saw that Daniel and his friends refused to eat the king's food, asking for permission to maintain their simpler diet of vegetables. They received permission to do so but only for a few days when they would be evaluated to determine if their diet was indeed superior to the one at the king's training center. Let's look at the rest of the story from there.

IT WORKED

Daniel's experiment of not eating the king's food produced good results:

> At the end of the ten days they looked healthier and better nourished than any of the young men who ate the royal food. So the guard took away their choice food and the wine they were to drink and gave them vegetables instead. To these four young men God gave knowledge and understanding of all kinds of literature and learning. And Daniel could understand visions and dreams of all kinds. At the end of the time set by the king to bring them into his service, the chief official presented them to Nebuchadnezzar. The king talked with them, and he found none equal to Daniel,

Hananiah, Mishael and Azariah; so they entered the king's service. In every matter of wisdom and understanding about which the king questioned them, he found them ten times better than all the magicians and enchanters in his whole kingdom. And Daniel remained there until the first year of King Cyrus (Daniel 1:15-21).

Daniel proved that his diet and way of life were superior to that of the Babylonians, and the king's official, who wanted results, was only too glad to comply. Not only did Daniel and his friends look better than the other young captives, they also outperformed their peers. Since God promotes people who develop their potential and not those who only have it but do nothing with it, it was only a matter of time before these men were noticed and given more responsibility.

MORE PROOF

There are many places in the Bible where the success of God's people is promised or at least insinuated. Here are a few:

- Do you see someone skilled in their work? They will serve before kings; they will not serve before officials of low rank (Proverbs 22:29).

- The Lord will make you the head, not the tail. If you pay attention to the commands of the Lord your God that I give you this day and carefully follow them, you will always be at the top, never at the bottom (Deuteronomy 28:13).

- Blessed is the one who does not walk in step with the wicked or stand in the way that sinners take or sit in the company of mockers, but whose delight is in the law of the Lord, and who meditates on his law day and night. That person is like a tree planted by streams of water, which yields its fruit in season and whose leaf does not wither—whatever they do prospers (Psalm 1:1-3).

In my busy days doing prison ministry, I would encourage the inmates to be true to their Christian values, for God watched and worked even in prison settings, just like He did in Babylon. There were times when God tested the inmates by giving them lowly positions or harsh overseers, but I never saw it fail that if they were true to God's ways and persevered, God would protect, promote, and prosper them. The same is true for you, no matter what situation you find yourself in.

While we must be careful not to worship at the altar of success, we must also acknowledge that God's ways work, and, if we follow them, He will exalt us in whatever sphere He calls us to serve. Therefore, if you are not advancing, you must ask the reasons why and examine yourself to see if you are the problem (you may choose not to advance or take on more responsibility, which is a whole other discussion). Are you bearing fruit? Do you have favor with those over you? Do you expect to be promoted or successful where you are? Do you care? If you have leadership power, do you champion the cause of those who are faithful, skilled, and honest? *Success in Babylon* is no different than anywhere else, for God is the same no matter where His people are called to live and serve.

CHAPTER FIVE

SUFFERING IN BABYLON

Let's review what we have learned so far in our *Success in Babylon* discussions. Our focus for the series is Daniel in Babylon to learn how we can be as successful in our spiritually-hostile environment as he was in his. To date, we have learned that:

1. Daniel was in Babylon not by choice, but by conscription.

2. Daniel and his friends had a bright future in front of them in Judah, but it suddenly changed and they had no say in the matter.

3. When they got to Babylon, they were given new names, transformed into eunuchs, and forced to assimilate into a new culture.

4. Even through all their suffering, Daniel and his entourage refused to eat the king's food, staying true to their heritage and values as Hebrew men.

5. God blessed their commitment and they were promoted into the king's service because God's ways always ultimately lead to success and promotion.

If we didn't learn anything else, we would have

plenty to think and pray about. There is more to learn, however, so let's move on to see what this chapter's lesson will be.

DRINK THE CUP

Before we move on to Daniel 2 in the next chapter, I want to look at one more concept in Daniel 1, which is one that is implied but not specifically mentioned. The concept is suffering. We already looked at Daniel 1:8, "But Daniel resolved not to defile himself with the royal food and wine, and he asked the chief official for permission not to defile himself this way." It would be simple to read through Daniel 1 and not take a moment to reflect on what these young exiles experienced emotionally to get to Babylon.

These young men had seen their homeland and Temple invaded and destroyed by foreigners—things some false prophets had predicted would never happen. Perhaps they saw their families killed, or they at least were separated from their loved ones when they were taken to Babylon, never to see them again. These captives had to walk the 600 miles to Babylon from Judea and were probably not given the best of treatment. All these events would add up to significant trauma that they would have remembered for the rest of their lives and it could have impacted them in a negative way.

In the midst of all that, they refused to drink wine from the king's cup because, they had their own cup to drink from—the cup of suffering. Jesus had His own cup of suffering to drink from and He implied that anyone who followed Him would have their own cup as well:

> Then the mother of Zebedee's sons came
> to Jesus with her sons and, kneeling down,
> asked a favor of him. "What is it you want?"
> he asked. She said, "Grant that one of these

two sons of mine may sit at your right and the other at your left in your kingdom." "You don't know what you are asking," Jesus said to them, "Can you drink the cup I am going to drink?" "We can," they answered. Jesus said to them, "*You will indeed drink from my cup*, but to sit at my right or left is not for me to grant. These places belong to those for whom they have been prepared by my Father" (Matthew 20:19-23, emphasis added).

Later, Jesus addressed His cup of suffering in the Garden of Gethsemane: "Going a little farther, he fell with his face to the ground and prayed, 'My Father, if it is possible, may this cup be taken from me. Yet not as I will, but as you will'" (Matthew 26:39). The cup was a reference to the agonizing suffering Jesus was about to endure, and Jesus knew it was going to be a struggle even for Him. Yet He endured and we are instructed to do the same:

> Therefore, since we are surrounded by such a great cloud of witnesses, let us throw off everything that hinders and the sin that so easily entangles. And let us run with perseverance the race marked out for us, fixing our eyes on Jesus, the pioneer and perfecter of faith. For the joy set before him he endured the cross, scorning its shame, and sat down at the right hand of the throne of God. Consider him who endured such opposition from sinners, so that you will not grow weary and lose heart (Hebrews 12:1-3).

GET READY

When I used to speak in prison settings, I reminded the inmates that part of their lot was suffering, something many of them had either experienced in their lives or committed crimes to avoid (the suffering that is). Either way, they were going to have to deny themselves, pick up their crosses, and follow His example—and that was going to cause them to suffer. The same is true for you regardless of what situation you find yourself. If you are going to fulfill your life purpose and be true to the Lord's will, you will suffer. Paul understood this and rejoiced in the privilege to do so: "Now I rejoice in what I am suffering for you, and I fill up in my flesh what is still lacking in regard to Christ's afflictions, for the sake of his body, which is the church" (Colossians 1:24).

Daniel was successful in his Babylon because he embraced suffering and did not allow it to deter him from serving God. He was not bitter and he willingly gave the best of who he was to his captors, as we will see in later chapters. Can you do the same? Can you give your best to your Babylon as you serve your Nebuchadnezzar? Can you follow Christ not only when the blessings flow, but also when the sufferings abound? I close with this admonition from Hebrews:

> Remember those earlier days after you had received the light, when you endured in a great conflict full of suffering. Some. times you were publicly exposed to insult and persecution; at other times you stood side by side with those who were so treated. You suffered along with those in prison and joyfully accepted the confiscation of your property, because you knew that you yourselves had better and lasting possessions. So do not throw away your confidence; it will be richly rewarded. You need to persevere so that when you have done the will of God, you will receive what he

has promised. For, "In just a little while, he who is coming will come and will not delay." And, "But my righteous one will live by faith. And I take no pleasure in the one who shrinks back." But we do not belong to those who shrink back and are destroyed, but to those who have faith and are saved (Hebrews 10:32-39).

As you work or live in Babylon, I pray you also will not shrink back but will embrace and rejoice in the suffering that is yours, that is making up what is lacking in Christ's suffering, as Paul wrote:

Now I rejoice in what I am suffering for you, and I fill up in my flesh what is still lacking in regard to Christ's afflictions, for the sake of his body, which is the church (Colossians 1:24).

CHAPTER SIX

DOING THE IMPOSSIBLE IN BABYLON

In this chapter, let's look at Daniel after he and his friends were promoted having distinguished themselves during their time of training. No sooner had they been recognized for superior service when they had to face another crisis:

> In the second year of his reign, Nebuchadnezzar had dreams; his mind was troubled and he could not sleep. So the king summoned the magicians, enchanters, sorcerers and astrologers to tell him what he had dreamed. When they came in and stood before the king, he said to them, "I have had a dream that troubles me and I want to know what it means." Then the astrologers answered the king, 'May the king live forever! Tell your servants the dream, and we will interpret it." The king replied to the astrologers, "This is what I have firmly decided: If you do not tell me what my dream was and interpret it, I will have you cut into pieces and your houses turned into piles of rubble. But if you tell me the dream and explain it, you will receive from me gifts and rewards and great honor. So

21

tell me the dream and interpret it for me."

Once more they replied, "Let the king tell his servants the dream, and we will interpret it." Then the king answered, "I am certain that you are trying to gain time, because you realize that this is what I have firmly decided: If you do not tell me the dream, there is only one penalty for you. You have conspired to tell me misleading and wicked things, hoping the situation will change. So then, tell me the dream, and I will know that you can interpret it for me." The astrologers answered the king, "There is no one on earth who can do what the king asks! No king, however great and mighty, has ever asked such a thing of any magician or enchanter or astrologer. What the king asks is too difficult. No one can reveal it to the king except the gods, and they do not live among humans" (Daniel 2:1-11).

Nebuchadnezzar was a difficult man to work with and for. He obviously had a short fuse on a bad temper, and he had high expectations for his advisors and officials. No one believed his standards could be achieved, and they were all about to get permanently "fired" for their inability to measure up.

DANIEL TO THE RESCUE

Daniel was included in the king's death edict, but when faced with this dilemma, he did not panic or try to escape. He simply applied his faith in God, right there in Babylon, on behalf of a heathen king and empire that had done him and his friends much harm:

When Arioch, the commander of the king's guard, had gone out to put to death the wise men of Babylon, Daniel spoke to

him with wisdom and tact. He asked the
king's officer, "Why did the king issue such
a harsh decree?" Arioch then explained the
matter to Daniel, At this, Daniel went in
to the king and asked for time, so that he
might interpret the dream for him (Daniel
2:14-16).

Daniel believed that his God could perform
the impossible, but it wasn't just something he talked
or sang choruses about. Daniel acted on his faith and
saved not only his life, but also the lives of the other wise men, most of them engaged in practices like
sooth-saying, consulting the dead, and sorcery all practices prohibited by Daniel's God. Of course, we know
the outcome:

Then Daniel returned to his house and explained the matter to his friends Hananiah,
Mishael and Azariah. He urged them to
plead for mercy from the God of heaven
concerning this mystery, so that he and his
friends might not be executed with the rest
of the wise men of Babylons During the
night the mystery was revealed to Daniel in
a vision (Daniel 2:17-19a).

It is remarkable that Daniel received not just
the king's dream interpretation, but also had the exact
same dream. How did Daniel know he had the correct
dream? How was he so sure? He was confident because
he was an Old Testament man living in New Testament
truth:

Consider it pure joy, my brothers and sis-
ters, whenever you face trials of many
kinds, because you know that the testing of
your faith produces perseverance. Let perseverance finish its work so that you may be

mature and complete, not lacking anything. If any of you lacks wisdom, you should ask God, who gives generously to all without finding fault, and it will be given to you. But when you ask, you must believe and not doubt, because the one who doubts is like a wave of the sea, blown and tossed by the wind. That person should not expect to receive anything from the Lord. Such a person is double-minded and unstable in all they do (James 1:2-8).

THE LESSONS

If you are in Babylon, you can trust God to act according to your faith, even if you are serving what seems to be a secular or non-Christian entity. God responds to faith, and God still does the impossible, but usually for those who trust and ask Him to do so. What's more, God can assign you to express your purpose and faith in a setting that is less than ideal, a place not of your choosing or liking.

I would tell the inmates in prison that God wanted them to express the best of who they were for guards and authorities who were sometimes harsh and demeaning. And while most inmates declared their innocence, I know there were a few who were indeed innocent but still serving time. What's more, God expected them to be involved in making their Babylon a better place to live and work, and God expects the same of you, no matter how diff. cult your conditions or oversight.

Many saints tell me their favorite Bible verse is found in Philippians 4:13: "I can do all things through him who gives me strength." When they tell me that, I usually respond by asking,

"So what are some of the 'all things' you are

doing?"They usually look surprised, for they are stating that they can do all things, not that they are doing all things and there is a big difference, which distinguishes productive, doing Christians from non-productive, talk-only ones.

Are you giving your best in Babylon? Are you heeding God's directive in Jeremiah 29:7: "Also, seek the peace and prosperity of the city to which I have carried you into exile. Pray to the Lord for it, because if it prospers, you too will prosper"? Your "city" may be a place of business, a prison, a school, or even a church located in or around Babylon. Wherever it is, God is watching and waiting for you to get involved, and doesn't mind doing the impossible for His servants who ask and believe in the process. The problem is not whether or not God can do it, but whether His people are willing, He is, if you are, so in the coming days, find a place to insert your wisdom-giving God into your wisdom-starved Babylon and be the source of blessing for many who are as unworthy of that blessing now as you once were.

CHAPTER SEVEN

WORSHIP
IN BABYLON

In case you have forgotten, I am writing this book in response to a challenge from friends who heard me talk about teaching this material years ago when I was involved in prison ministry.

I accepted their challenge. While some of these messages were delivered to an audience of inmates, they are relevant for anyone who is serving the Lord in a spiritually hostile environment and this book includes many new messages I did not teach back in my prison-ministry days.

In the last chapter, we saw Daniel's faith when he asked the Lord to reveal to him the king's dreams along with their interpretation. No other wise man in Babylon thought this possible, but Daniel knew that his God majored in the impossible, so he did not hesitate to ask, expecting an answer: "At this, Daniel went in to the king and asked for time, so that he might interpret the dream for him" (Daniel 2:16). All the wise men were granted a reprieve from the king's death sentence, and Daniel and his friends went to work.

DANIEL WORSHIPPED

Even though Daniel expected God to answer his request, he was still overwhelmed with joy and gratitude when He did His first response was worship:

"Praise be to the name of God for ever

and ever, wisdom and power are his. He changes times and seasons; he deposes kings and raises up others. He gives wisdom to the wise and knowledge to the discerning. He reveals deep and hidden things; he knows what lies in darkness, and light dwells with him. 1 thank and praise you, God of my ancestors: You have given me wisdom and power, you have made known 'to me what we asked of you, you have made known to us the dream of the king" (Daniel 2:20-23).

It is one thing to worship God for who He is, and we should do that with intelligence and eloquence because He is a great God if He never does another thing for us. It is quite another thing to worship Him because of what He does for us, and we should be asking and expecting God to do marvelous things, even if we are serving Him in Babylon.

One time, I served on the board of directors for an organization whose finances were a mess. I offered to take the records and try to make sense out of them. The board agreed, so I took all the records, spread them out over a large table, and prayed, "Lord, You know where the money is and where I need to go." Immediately, found the trail of the missing, money. Guess what I did after that? I worshipped the Lord, thanking Him for His help.

Then I took my report to my fellow board members and they were all pleasantly surprised to hear what I had to say (there was no criminal activity; just bad record-keeping). Someone asked, "How did you find all this out so quickly?" My response was, " prayed."The members looked around at each other and nervously repeated, "He prayed. Yeah, right, he prayed," and then one person yelled out, "Well, praise the Lord!"

and everyone laughed to relieve the tension. That is exactly what happened when Daniel gave his report.

THE KING WORSHIPPED

When the king heard someone tell him both his dreams and their interpretation, he was amazed. What was his response? He worshipped:

> Then King Nebuchadnezzar fell prostrate before Daniel and paid him honor and ordered that an offering and incense be presented to him. The king said to Daniel, "Surely your God is the God of gods and the Lord of kings and a revealer of mysteries, for you were able to reveal this mystery" (Daniel 2:46-47).

When God sends us to Babylon, He desires that we represent Him well so that others will know and worship Him. Therefore, our goal in Babylon is worship (both personal and corporate) from both those who know Him and those who don't. When is the last time someone worshipped your God because of the job you did in Babylon?

The same thing happened when the Queen of Sheba came to visit Solomon. Like Nebuchadnezzar, she was overwhelmed by what she beheld from one of God's servants and said, "Praise be to the Lord your God, who has delighted in you and placed you on the throne of Israel. Because of the Lord's eternal love for Israel, he has made you king to maintain justice and righteousness" (1 Kings 10:9). This praise in or from Babylon is not only to be for who God is, but also for what He does. They will only see what He does when they behold the work we do and the attitude of joy we have as we represent Him—no matter how tough things get.

Are you in Babylon? Is your goal survival and

self-preservation, or is it worship? Are you expecting the impossible and then worshipping God when He delivers it? Are you serving the heathen "kings" in your assigned sphere and causing them to think about and maybe even worship your God? I hope you are, but it's not too late to do so if you're not. simply change your mindset from that of being a prisoner to being a servant of God who willingly chooses (even if you are bound and chained) to do His will. When you do, God will enhance your worship and that of those around you when you show forth the glories of His love and grace in the work that you produce.

CHAPTER EIGHT

PROMOTION IN BABYLON

In this chapter, let's go back and reexamine Daniel's promotion to be the chief of all the wise men and see what lessons we can learn from it to help us today.

MODERN BABYLON

We have entered a world that is similar to Daniel's world in Babylon, which is the reason I am studying his life to see how we can survive and thrive in a spiritually-hostile environment. like he did. Babylon was a magnificent city and culture. It had massive buildings, a strong economy, and because of its military conquests, a diverse culture made up of the many people Babylon had conquered. When Daniel arrived, he had come from a culture where everyone thought, worshipped, and worked the same. In Babylon, Daniel was only one voice among many, and that is the situation the church finds itself in today.

There was a time when the church was the dominant and main, if not the only voice, in Western cultures. Now that's changed, and believers don't quite know what to do. In a sense, the Church and its members have retreated, hoping and waiting for a revival or reversal that may never come so they can regain their dominant voice. That is why we as individuals, and the Church in general, needs to study how to survive in a world hostile to spiritual things, and that is why Daniel is the perfect role model. We must now be content with influence because there are many voices vying for the hearts and minds of people.

We passed over rather quickly that after his interview with the king and then his interpretation of the king's dream, Daniel was promoted to be over all the wise men of Babylon (see Daniel 2:48). Think about that. Daniel has responsibility to oversee the soothsayers, necromancers, magicians, sorcerers, and conjurers in the realm. What were those business meetings like? "We will now hear a report from the sorcerers in south Babylon to hear what they are conjuring up these days." This was nothing like what Daniel had grown up with in Judea.

A CHANCE TO SERVE

When no one could interpret the king's dream after first telling the king what his dream was, the king ordered all these wise men to be put to death, including Daniel and his friends, Daniel's attitude could have been, "Good. They are all a bunch of sinners doing things Yahweh forbids. I didn't want to be here in the first place, so if we all die, we die." Instead, Daniel intervened and saved all their lives. He was not bitter and did not have a victim's mentality, or an attitude that said, "Uh, this is not in my job description and is above my pay scale. Sorry."

This is the reason we chose Daniel when we taught inmates, for their prison environment was similar to Babylon. We encouraged them not to sit out their sentence playing cards or pool. We urged them not to just to survive but thrive by finding opportunities to display excellence in their work and behavior. Many of the guards harassed them, but we taught them to submit to unfair treatment with joy and patience. Some of the inmates were promoted to positions of significance and trust because they learned how to exist and prosper in their Babylon. It may be time for you to do the same.

If your purpose is expressed and fulfilled in the Church, that's great and you have important work. Most people's purpose and creativity, however, are not expressed in church but in the spiritually-neutral (or worse) spheres of business, education, the military, or social work. If we learn to do what Daniel did and, more importantly, be who Daniel was, then we will be promoted in Babylon, just like he was: "The Lord will make you the head, not the tail. If you pay attention to the commands of the Lord your God that I give you this day and carefully follow them, you will always be at the top, never at the bottom" (Deuteronomy 28:13).

THE EARTH IS THE LORD'S

The Lord was the one who orchestrated Daniel's relocation to Babylon, just like He did Joseph's to Egypt. And there is a good chance God has you where you are for a purpose, and it's not just to work out something in your heart. God wants you to give the best of who you are and who He made you to be to Babylon because He loves all His creation. He has sent you because He is reaching out to the Babylonians and is taking care of His creation: "The earth is the Lord's, and everything in it, the world, and all who live in it; for he founded it on the seas and established it on the waters" (Psalm 24:1). God cares about Babylon and because He does, He assigned you a place there. You are not to tolerate that position, you are to celebrate it and represent the Lord well.

God took some of His best and gave them an assignment in Babylon, where there was great danger and risk. They accepted their lot and God was with them. They were never totally in sync with Babylon and faced harassment and persecution their entire stay, but God preserved them and they continued to excel and stay true to their values. The same may be true for you, and it will be important for you to keep your eyes on the prize of the words, "Well done, good and faithful servant" as you serve your time in Babylon, not because you have done something wrong, but because God had a purpose for you being there.

CHAPTER NINE
LEADERSHIP IN BABYLON

In the previous chapter, we saw that Daniel was given a chance to serve, with God's help, in Babylon, which had tried to assimilate him and his friends into their culture for their own purposes. God had His own reasons for sending Daniel there and He revealed Himself and His will in a setting where the Jewish people would never have chosen to be. Let's look at that more closely, for you also may be in a place where you question the venue for God's assignment for you at this time.

THE KING'S DREAM

Nebuchadnezzar was not a God-fearing or God-worshipping man, yet God chose to put him on the throne:

> "This was the dream, and now we will in-
> terpret it to the king. Your Majesty, you are
> the king of kings. The God of heaven has
> given you dominion and power and might
> and glory; in your hands he has placed all
> mankind and the beasts of the field and the
> birds in the sky. Wherever they live, he has
> made you ruler over them all. You are that
> head of gold" (Daniel 2:36-38).

Daniel clearly understood that God had put Nebuchadnezzar in charge, and Daniel's role was not to oppose him, but rather to serve him. Daniel had no ego that drove him to be the main leader, and he was humble enough to submit to God's choice, even though the king was not part of Daniel's world. When I worked in prison settings, I tried to help the prisoners recognize and submit to authority, not because the authority was perfect, but because God had placed them there.

I learned this lesson once when I had a job and was placed under a man who had serious moral issues. I was young in the Lord and not aware of my attitude, but God knew. When my finances dried up and I sought the Lord for the reason, He revealed that my lack was due to my disrespect for my supervisor.

I cried out to God, "I am serving You. Why are you picking on me? My boss is the one with the sin problem!" Yet God taught me that how I served that boss was an indication of how I would serve Him, using First Peter 2:18 to admonish me: "Servants, be submissive to your masters with all respect, not only to those who are good and gentle, but also to those who are unreasonable" (NASB). The NASB version has a footnote by the word unreasonable that indicates another acceptable translation for the word is perverse. My overseer was perverse, but God wanted me to serve him because He had sent me to my own Babylon. Daniel came to the same conclusion concerning his Babylon.

GOD SPOKE TO HIM

Not only did God place Nebuchadnezzar where he was, but God spoke to him and used Daniel to deliver the message:

> Daniel replied, "No wise man, enchanter, magician or diviner can explain to the king the mystery he has asked about, but there is a God in heaven who reveals mysteries. He has shown King Nebuchadnezzar what

will happen in days to come. Your dream and the visions that passed through your mind as you were lying in bed are these" (Daniel 2:27-28).

If Daniel had received the dream, no one would have paid attention to it or its meaning. Because God works through leadership, however, He gave the king the dream and then the supernatural interpretation through Daniel so the king would know God had spoken to him. God not only assigns your purpose but where you will fulfill and express it. My purpose is relevant anywhere, but it is the most effective when I am in Africa.

We taught the inmates to assume that they were to fulfill their purpose in prison instead of waiting until they were released to serve God. God wanted to use them (and you) to reveal His will to Babylon, and He doesn't need permission or doesn't have to explain His reasons for using anyone to do so. When I realized that God has sent me to the place with the "perverse" supervisor, I surrendered to His will, asked Him to help me adjust my attitude, and determined I would stay there the rest of my life if that was what He wanted. Lo and behold, that job and that supervisor were my springboard to ministry.

When God adjusted my perspective on leadership and His role in it, He was free to promote me to other situations where I could serve His purpose not just for the Church, but also for the world at large— and for leaders who were less than godly (in both the church and the world).

Are you in Babylon? Are you chafing under the leadership of someone who is ungodly? Do you resent being there, and are holding back your gifts and purpose? If you see that God has assigned you where you are, you can thrive and prosper even in the worst

36

of environments. When you see that God wants you to serve the leadership where you are, God is free to use you to speak to those leaders on His behalf, and who knows, God may reveal His mysteries to you in a place not of your choosing while He works out your purpose after the fashion of His will.

CHAPTER TEN

FIRED IN BABYLON

The story of Daniel's long and successful career in Babylon is important for us to study, for he modeled how to be faithful to the Lord in a hostile spiritual environment. This is something believers must learn to do in our world or risk retreating into a spiritual ghetto where it is safe but cut off from the people who desperately need to hear about and know the Lord. In this chapter, let's move on to Daniel 3, which contains the famous story of Daniel's three friends and their encounter with a fiery furnace. I suggest you read the story before you go on.

FIRED

Even though he was only the head of gold in his dream, the king ordered a huge statue of gold be made of his likeness and further commanded all his subjects to worship the image. If there was one thing that was especially abhorrent to a Jew, it was idolatry, so it is not surprising that Daniel's friends refused to bow down before the statue, and let their refusal be known to all. Their rivals, seeing a chance to knock the Jews from their leadership perch, reported this to the king, who was filled with rage:

> Furious with rage, Nebuchadnezzar summoned Shadrach, Meshach and Abednego. So these men were brought before the king, and Nebuchadnezzar said to them, "Is it true, Shadrach, Meshach and Abednego, that you do not serve my gods or worship

the image of gold I have set up? Now when
you hear the sound of the horn, flute, zith-
er, lyre, harp, pipe and all kinds of music, if
you are ready to fall down and worship the
image 1 made, very good. But if you do not
worship it, you will be thrown immediately into a blazing furnace. Then what god
will be able to rescue you from my hand?"
(Daniel 3:13-15).

When the three men stood their ground, the
king decided to "fire" them on the spot by throwing
them into a blazing furnace. What was the purpose
for this furnace? The Middle East is a hot place, yet
there was a furnace that the king ordered to be heat-
ed seven times hotter than usual. I would assume this
furnace was for sacrifice, and I would also assume the
three men were not the first to be thrown into that
fiery grave. This then became a confrontation between
the God of the three men and the idols of Babylon,
something akin to the meeting between Elijah and the
prophets of Baal in First Kings 18.

SUBMISSION, NOT OBEDIENCE

The three men submitted to the king, which
we are commanded to do as believers, but they did not
obey the king—and there is a difference. Submission
is an attitude and the three men were willing to submit to the consequences of their decision They did not
scream at the king or threaten him with divine retri-
bution. They simply said, "You have the authority from
God to do what you are going to do. We recognize
your authority and will submit to it but we cannot
obey you."

When we taught these principles in a prison setting, we urged the men and women to maintain a respectful attitude and submit to the authorities

without obeying them if they gave an order that was contrary to God's will or illegal. If they were ordered to lie or cheat, they could not obey but then had to submit to the consequences for their choices with a godly attitude—just as Jesus did when He was condemned to death. He submitted to Pilate and the authorities, all the while obeying the Father, who was the higher authority.

What happened to the three men? Even though they were "fired," they met the Lord in the midst of their flames. Not only that, but the things that had bound them were burned off and they were freed to walk around in the fire. It is of note that when they were freed from their restraints, they did not run out of the furnace. They had to be called out by the king and when they came out, they did not even smell like smoke.

Are you serving in Babylon? Are you being asked to compromise what you know is righteous but are afraid to disobey because you may lose your job or reputation? Are you giving in to peer pressure to be like everyone else in your Babylon? Is the king's anger intimidating you and causing you to camouflage your faithful witness? If you have asked the Lord to be closer to Him, is it possible that you must enter your own fiery furnace to meet Him there?

Babylon has many fiery furnaces and many kings with an anger problem. I urge you to focus on the King of kings and determine to be faithful to Him while the many other kings in Babylon vie for your heart and affection. If you remain faithful, you will be a worthy servant of the Most High even if you get "fired" for your righteousness.

CHAPTER ELEVEN
INFLUENCE IN BABYLON

Let's move on to Daniel 4 where Nebuchadnezzar, king of Babylon, told us his own story of his encounter with the "Most High God," to use his own terminology. So far, we have seen that Nebuchadnezzar was the king who conquered Jude and brought Daniel and his friends to Babylon. While he was at it, he also conquered much of the known world at that time, and he acted like a man who was used to getting his own way on his terms. We have. read about the king's dream, Daniel's interpretation, the golden statue, and the king having Daniel's friends thrown into the fiery furnace (and surviving). Nebuchadnezzar played a central role in all these stories. In chapter four, we read the following account from the king:

> King Nebuchadnezzar, to the nations and peoples of every language, who live in all the earth: May you prosper greatly! It is my pleasure to tell you about the miraculous signs and wonders that the Most High God has performed for me. How great are his signs, how mighty his wonders! His kingdom is an eternal kingdom; his dominion endures from generation to generation. 1, Nebuchadnezzar, was at home in my palace, contented and prosperous. I had a dream that made me afraid. As I was lying

in bed, the images and visions that passed through my mind terrified me. So I commanded that all the wise men of Babylon be brought before me to interpret the dream for me. When the magicians, enchanters, astrologers and diviners came, I told them the dream, but they could not interpret it for me. Finally, Daniel came into my presence and I told him the dream. (He is called Belteshazzar, after the name of my god, and the spirit of the holy gods is in him) (Daniel 4:1-8).

Let's examine that passage more closely.

GOD TALK

As I have pointed out, Babylon was a place where there was what's called a mixed bag of spirituality. There were lots of gods, philosophies, religious and spiritual practices, and idolatry. The name Babylon is used five times in the book of Revelation, always to denote spiritual uncleanness and wickedness: "With a mighty voice he shouted: "'Fallen! Fallen is Babylon the Great!' She has become a dwelling for demons and a haunt for every impure spirit, a haunt for every unclean bird, a haunt for every unclean and detestable animal" (Revelation 18:2). Yet God transferred Daniel and his friends to this wicked and idolatrous city under a wicked and idolatrous ruler to bear testimony to God's supremacy and sovereignty.

We will delve more deeply into Daniel 4 in subsequent chapters, but right now I want you to see what it took for Daniel to be successful in Babylon. Daniel had to be content with influence, for he was not going to "convert" the king to Judaism, Instead, Daniel introduced the king to his God, who unbeknownst to the king was also his God. God partnered with Daniel and worked to bring the king to a place of humility and revelation. Even when that happened, the king's "God talk" was a mixture of his knowledge of the true God coupled with his devotion to his personal Babylonian god.

THE MIXED BAG

I mentioned that Babylon was a mixed bag when it came to spirituality. God had His witnesses there, but they functioned in the midst of wise men involved in all manner of forbidden spiritual practice. Yet that did not keep God from revealing Himself, Notice that the king referred to Jehovah as "the Most High God" in verse two but then referred to his personal god, Bel, in verse eight when he referenced Daniel's Babylonian name, Belteshazzar. It appears that the king accepted Daniel's god as the chief God while clinging to the worship of what he considered a lesser god.

Daniel's role in Babylon was to influence those around him, and the same is true for those of us called to serve in modern Babylon. When I worked with inmates, I urged them not to feel like a failure if their witnessing fell short and people refused to convert and be baptized, for God's purpose may be something beyond individual salvations. God also wants to help His people influence those around them to make godly decisions and live more holy lives. We saw corrupt guards begin to change their behaviors and also saw inmates influence (for the good) prison policies and practices.

While we have the same objective as God's "who wants all people to be saved and to come to a knowledge of the truth" (1 Timothy 2:4), we must at times be content with doing what Daniel did: standing for the truth even though most will either ignore or oppose it. In Daniel's story, the one who was least likely to be influenced was (the king), and he became the first Gentile author in God's inspired word when he wrote what is now Daniel chapter four.

Are you in a place of influence even though you are in a spiritual environment that is a mixed bag of philosophies and practices? Are you content with influence while allowing God to use that influence to touch lives at a deeper level? Are you willing to sow seed and allow God to oversee the seed in the hearts of others, bringing it to harvest perhaps long after you are gone from that harvest field?

You need to have the right goal if you want to be successful in Babylon and that goal should be influence as an ambassador for the truth of God in Christ. If you do your part, then God will do His, and no king, not even the great Nebuchadnezzar, can withstand the grace of God when He decides to pour it out on any undeserving soul.

CHAPTER TWELVE

FORGIVENESS IN BABYLON

In the previous chapter, we looked at Daniel's leadership position in Babylon, which was one of influence and not control. While he had access to the king due to his high position, Daniel could not control anything or anyone, He could only influence them and their decisions through his godly presence, wisdom, and cooperation. He did influence the king to the point that the king was confronted with the reality of Daniel's God being "the Most High God," but the king maintained loyalty to his Babylonian gods as well.

Daniel was a remarkable young man, on par with Joseph, for they both served pagan kings in heathen cultures and did so with distinction and grace. That is what it will take (grace) for us to serve in our Babylon, which is an accurate description for the modern world. That is the reason we are studying Daniel, so we can extract the lessons to not only to survive our stint in Babylon but to thrive there:

In this chapter, let's look at an essential attitude Daniel had to have if he was going to prosper and be God's agent in Babylon, and that attitude (or behavior) was forgiveness.

LEST WE OVERLOOK THE FACTS

It is important that we not romanticize Daniel's relocation to and tour of duty in Babylon. Let's review what we know or can surmise. Daniel was there against his will. He was a prisoner or detainee of war, carried off to Babylon in a massive relocation program designed to obliterate his nation and people by having them assimilate into the dominant Babylonian culture. He had seen his home city of Jerusalem ransacked and destroyed. Perhaps his family was carried off with him or more probably killed. His future was radically altered from what he imagined it to be, and he was forced to learn a new language and culture, while chosen (without his consent) to serve in the king's court. This was the same king who designed and led everything that Daniel had been through, which included ordering the unsuccessful execution of Daniel along with his three friends as described in Daniel 1 through 3.

We cannot forget what Daniel went through as we approach Daniel 4 and read how the king called on Daniel to interpret yet another dream. We would understand if Daniel was suffering from Post-Traumatic Stress Syndrome after all he had been through. We could identify with his decision if he had chosen to have no part in assisting or comforting the enemy of his people: Yet Daniel performed nobly and well in Babylon and he could do so because he had learned to forgive his enemies and make peace with God's plan for his life.

TO YOUR ADVERSARIES

How do we know that Daniel forgave the king and his captors? Let's read one verse that describes Daniel's disposition toward those among whom he was forced to live and work:

> Then Daniel (also called Belteshazzar) was greatly perplexed for a time, and his thoughts terrified him. So the king said, "Belteshazzar, do not let the dream or its meaning alarm you." Belteshazzar answered,

"My lord, if only the dream applied to your enemies and its meaning to your adversaries!" (Daniel 4:19, emphasis added).

There are two options to explain Daniel's response when he heard the king's dream. He was either being polite and deceptive, hiding his true feelings because he was in the presence of the king who could take off his head, or Daniel had made peace with his purpose and had forgiven the king and his people. I choose to believe it was the latter. Daniel had forgiven those who had done him wrong and thus was in a position to utilize his spiritual gifts and divine wisdom to benefit or at least advise the king. That is remarkable.

I had a supervisor once who was nothing short of a rascal. He lied to me on numerous occasions, did not follow through on promised raises, paid me half-time instead of time-and-a-half for overtime, and stole from me and others. Then one day, my own finances were drying up (I was paid by commission at the time) and when I sought the Lord, He revealed my leanness was due to my unforgiveness toward that man. I cried out, "Why are you picking on me? I'm not the one with the moral problem; he is!" God would not relent and I learned an important lesson that God expected me to do right and be a servant to others regardless of their worthiness or how tough I thought I had it.

That is a lesson we tried to impart to the inmates when I was involved in prison ministry. They had to forgive those who had betrayed, disappointed, abandoned, or despitefully used them and often there were many they had to forgive. They included police, attorneys, guards, lovers, family, children, spouses, themselves, and even God. Their forgiveness was not to be given according to the response of those being forgiven, but in response to God's will:

> Be kind and compassionate to one another, forgiving each other, just as in Christ God forgave you. Follow God's example, therefore, as dearly loved children and walk in the way of love, just as Christ loved us and gave himself up for us as a fragrant offering and sacrifice to God (Ephesians 4:32-5:2).

We taught them that they could not truly serve another person unless they had dealt with everything they held against them. We also helped them understand that forgiveness is often progressive, which meant they would forgive at a certain level and move on, only to confront deeper levels of bitterness and anger at a later time. They then had to repeat the process.

THE PRICE OF SUCCESS

Do you really want to succeed and not just exist in your Babylon? Have you made peace with those who wrongfully used you? Have you forgiven them to the extent that you can do them good, just like Daniel did in Babylon? Your purpose and creativity are not your own; God gave them to you and wants to direct how they are used.

If you have not forgiven, however, it is like a knot in a garden hose. The water may be running but it can't get past the knot, and your purpose is the same. It cannot get past the knot of unforgiveness. When I forgave my boss, my finances were restored and 1later realized he was part of my seminary training for the minis. try, for he taught me lessons no classroom could impart.

I pray that you will make the most of your lessons too so you can take your place on a Babylonian stage as a main actor in a purpose play that was written, directed, and produced just for you.

CHAPTER THIRTEEN
DEMOTED
IN BABYLON

If you are like most people, your first thought if you are looking for a job is that you need an organization—a company, a ministry, a social service organization to hire you. Then you pretty much expect to work there for a long time and if you are released or phased out, it can create waves of fear and depression, and then you start the process all over again.

There is nothing wrong with this, and God may use a company to take care of you-but He doesn't need one. He can take care of you all by Himself. What's more, God is your job counselor and can open and close doors in order to position you where He wants you to be. Daniel found all this to be true in Babylon as we will see in this chapter's lesson.

THE WRITING'S ON THE WALL

Nebuchadnezzar, Daniel and Judah's nemesis, eventually succumbed to death, as all kings and leaders do:"Do not put your trust in princes, in human beings, who cannot save. When their spirit departs, they return to the ground; on that very day their plans come to nothing" (Psalm 146:4-5). He was replaced on the throne by his son, Belshazzar, who was as arrogant and proud as his father had been, perhaps even more so:

> King Belshazzar gave a great banquet for
> a thousand of his nobles and drank wine
> with them. While Belshazzar was drinking

his wine, he gave orders to bring in the gold and silver goblets that Nebuchadnezzar his father had taken from the temple in Jerusalem, and the king and his nobles, his wives and his concubines drank from them. As they drank the wine, they praised the gods of gold and silver, of bronze, iron, wood and stone. Suddenly the fingers of a human hand appeared and wrote on the plaster of the wall, near the lampstand in the royal palace. The king watched the hand as it wrote. His face turned pale and he was so frightened that his legs became weak and his knees were knocking (Daniel 5:1-6).

There is a saying that "the writing's on the wall," and it means that things are not going well and is about to end—and the saying came from this story.

This scenario has always fascinated me when I try to imagine the scene. What did the fingers look like? What was the skin color? What did they write with? What were the reactions of the guests? Did they run? We know the reaction of the king, for he was terrified. Obviously, God knew how to get His message across in a manner and in the language that got everyone's attention.

Yet my question to you is this: *Where was Daniel when all this was happening?*

THE LORD TAKETH AWAY

The answer is that Daniel was nowhere to be found. After all his service to the king and Babylon, the new king had fired and demoted him, and he had every right to choose his own team of wise men and counselors. In choosing his team, however, he overlooked the best man in the kingdom, and what's more, in his time of trouble, the king did not even remember Daniel existed:

> The queen, hearing the voices of the king and his nobles, came into the banquet hall. "May the king live forever!" she said. "Don't be alarmed! Don't look so pale! There is a man in your kingdom who has the spirit of the holy gods in him. In the time of your father he was found to have insight and intelligence and wisdom like that of the gods. Your father, King Nebuchadnezzar, appointed him chief of the magicians, enchanters, astrologers and diviners" (Daniel 5:10-11).

The queen had to remind Belshazzar that Daniel was around and capable of helping interpret the writing. That is how far removed Daniel was from his once prominent role in the kingdom. We used to remind all the inmates in prison ministry that God was in control of their sentence and the jobs they had while incarcerated, and that would be the same, when they got out. They did not own their positions and what they had was by God's choice, not man's. We reminded them (and I remind you) of the oft-quoted verse from Job: "And said, 'Naked came I out of my mother's womb, and naked shall I return thither: the Lord gave, and the Lord hath taken away; blessed be the name of the Lord" (Job 1:21 KJV).

The king hastily summoned Daniel, who was immediately ushered into the party room to see if he could interpret the handwriting. Let's see how Daniel responded.

DANIEL TO THE RESCUE ... SORT OF

When the king asked Daniel for help, he could have said, "Why you little brat! I was serving your father when you were in diapers running around his throne. I didn't deserve to be demoted. You have treated me terribly. Read your own handwriting. I quit! And if you kill me, who cares. I am older now and lived a fuller life than Iever thought possible in this hell hole of a place."

That is not what Daniel did or said, for once again, he was magnanimous in service, knowing he was there as God's representative and not as an independent contractor: "Then Daniel answered the king, You may keep your gifts for yourself and give your rewards to someone else. Nevertheless. I will read the writing for the king and tell him what it means" (Daniel 5:17).

Of course, the message on the wall was not good for the king, for God was about to "taketh away" his throne and life: "Here is what these words mean: Mene: God has numbered the days of your reign and brought it to an end. Tekel: You have been weighed on the scales and found wanting. Peres: Your kingdom is divided and given to the Medes and Persians" (Daniel 5:26-28). And that is exactly what happened, for the king was assassinated that very night. Daniel was the only one who could interpret the strange writing because he was the only one in touch with the living God, and the same may be true for you in your life situation.

Are you in Babylon? Have you been unfairly treated? Are you angry? Have you decided to withhold the best of who you are and what you can do? Do you think God needs a king or the world system to care for you or to make a place for you? Are people who wronged you now looking to you for help? The verse from Iob is as pertinent and relevant for you as it was for Daniel, for God in His infinite wisdom opens and closes doors, promotes and demotes, and uses and retires, as He sees fit. Even though you are in Babylon with all its enterprise and wealth, you are still God's child and He is the best Father in the universe, even though at times He works with us in ways we cannot see or understand.

CHAPTER FOURTEEN

PRIDE AND HUMILITY IN BABYLON

I have walked with the Lord for more than 46 years and I have learned many important lessons and one of them is this: If you want to get God's attention, do one of two things either be proud or be humble. Let's look at some biblical justification for stating this truth:

- For though the Lord is exalted, Yet He regards the lowly, but the haughty He knows from afar (Psalm 138:6).

- "The fear of the Lord is to hate evil; Pride and arrogance and the evil way and the perverted mouth, I hate" (Proverbs 8:13).

- There are six things the Lord hates, seven that are detestable to him: haughty eyes, a lying tongue, and hands that shed innocent blood (Proverbs 6:16-17).

- He mocks proud mockers but shows favor to the humble and oppressed (Proverbs 3:34) (this verse is often quoted in the New Testament).

- For the Lord of hosts will have a day of reckoning against everyone who is proud and lofty and against everyone who is lifted up, that he may be abased (Isaiah 2:12).

- "He has done mighty deeds with His arm; He has scattered those who were proud in the thoughts of their "heart" (Luke 1:51, spoken by Mary, the mother of Jesus).

What does this have to do with Success in Babylon? It is important because we see this truth play out in the lives of both Daniel and Nebuchadnezzar, and God may be "playing it out" in your life as well.

THE KING

Nebuchadnezzar was a proud, hot-tempered, and ruthless fellow. When Daniel delivered the interpretation to his first dream in which the king was the head of gold, he decided to build a statue of gold, focusing on himself as if he was the only character featured in the dream—which he was not. When Daniel's friends refused to bow down to his image, the king tried to execute them. God continued to reach out to the king, warning him through Daniel:

> "This is the interpretation, Your Majesty, and this is the decree the Most High has issued against my lord the king: You will be driven away from people and will live with the wild animals; you will eat grass like the ox and be drenched with the dew of heaven. Seven times will pass by for you until you acknowledge that the Most High is sovereign over all kingdoms on earth and gives them to anyone he wishes. The command to leave the stump of the tree with its roots means that your kingdom will be restored to you when you acknowledge that Heaven rules. Therefore, Your Majesty,

be pleased to accept my advice: Renounce your sins by doing what is right, and your wickedness by being kind to the oppressed. It may be that then your prosperity will continue" (Daniel 4:24-27).

The king had to humble himself or be humiliated and he chose the latter. For seven years, he acted like a beast (which is the end result of all human pride), until he acknowledged the truth of what Daniel had told him: "Now I, Nebuchadnezzar, praise and exalt and glorify the King of heaven, because everything he does is right and all his ways are just. And those who walk in pride he is able to humble" (Daniel 4:37).

THE POLAR OPPOSITE

On the other hand, Daniel was the polar opposite of the king—the epitome of humility, a superstar of spic proportions in the history of God's people, He accepted his relocation, his role in Babylon, and his forced servitude to a proud king with dignity and grace. He was an example of a truth that Jesus spoke 500 years after Daniel when He said, "For those who exalt themselves will be humbled, and those who humble themselves will be exalted" (Matthew 23:12),

When working with inmates, 1 detected a lot of pride in their lives and the lives of the officials around them, which was re markable, for some of them had nothing of which to be' proud, I taught them that God was humbling them, perhaps had even humiliated them, but regardless of which it was, they had to learn to cooperate with God's discipline. If they could do that, He would often exalt them like he did Daniel or restore them like he did Nebuchadnezzar, I also emphasized that their promotion was not a matter of humility only, for the Bible teaches that "No one from the east or the west or from the desert can exalt themselves,

It is God who judges: He brings one down, he exalts another" (Psalm 75:6-7). God will promote who He chooses to promote and it is best to humble one's self and accept His choices, for to resist is a form of pride.

If you are going to thrive in a spiritually-hostile environment, you must learn to walk in humility, not as an event but as a lifestyle. Determine to accept God's promise that He will respond to both humility and pride and choose the former as a means to activate God's favor and help. Not every story ends with the proud king being restored as this account relates, but the story shows what is important to God, and that means it should be our priority as well. Live by the words of Peter and you will prosper no matter where God places you: "Humble yourselves, therefore, under God's mighty hand, that he may lift you up in due time" (1 Peter 5:6).

CHAPTER FIFTEEN
EXCELLENCE IN BABYLON

In this chapter, let's look at Daniel's reinstatement to power and authority, this time under a new leader who had deposed the former Babylonian regime. The new king recognized talent and was quick to promote Daniel to his cabinet in one of the three highest positions in the land. Let's look at what other characteristics made Daniel so promotable on so many occasions under so many leaders.

NOT GOOD, BUT GREAT

We read this account of Daniel's reinstatement to a high position in Daniel 6:

> It pleased Darius to appoint 120 satraps to rule throughout the kingdom, with three administrators over them, one of whom was Daniel. The satraps were made accountable to them so that the king might not suffer loss. Now Daniel so distinguished himself among the administrators and the satraps by his exceptional qualities that the king planned to set him over the whole kingdom. At this, the administrators and the satraps tried to find grounds for charges against Daniel in his conduct of government affairs, but they were unable to do so. They could find no corruption in him, because he was trustworthy and

neither corrupt nor negligent. Finally these men said. "We will never find any basis for charges against this man Daniel unless it has something to do with the law of his God" (Daniel 1:1-5).

Daniel was promoted not because he was in the right place at the right time, or because he hung around long enough to climb the ladder of success. Daniel was promoted because he was not only good at what he did, Daniel was great at what he did. I have often said that God does not promote potential but promotes those who develop their potential. The potential is what God gives us but the development is what we do. The more skilled and cap. able we are, the higher the place God can send us.

When I was involved in prison ministry conducting The Lion's Den Seminar, I taught the inmates not to expect any promotion unless they had paid the price to produce excellence, regardless of the task. I had them look at, study, and apply Colossians 3:22-24:

> Slaves, obey your earthly masters in everything, and do it, not only when their eye is on you and to curry their favor, but with sincerity of heart and reverence for the Lord. Whatever you do, work at it with all your heart, as working for the Lord, not for human masters, since you know that you will receive an inheritance from the Lord as a reward. It is the Lord Christ you are serving.

That meant they had to humble themselves and do even menial tasks with great enthusiasm that produced excellent results not according to their standard but to the standard of others.

Yet there is one more important characteristic

that was present in Daniel's life and it is described in 6:4. "They could find no corruption in him, because he was trustworthy and neither corrupt nor negligent" (emphasis added). How can we label that trait that went along with Daniel's competence? Let's go there next.

INTEGRITY

Quite simply, Daniel had integrity, which one site defines as "the quality of being honest and having strong moral principles; moral uprightness." Daniel was trustworthy and Jesus outlined His interpretation of integrity and trustworthiness in Luke 16:10-12:

> "Whoever can be trusted with very little can also be trusted with much, and whoever is dishonest with very little will also be dishonest with much. So if you have not been trustworthy in handling worldly wealth, who will trust you with true riches? And if you have not been trustworthy with someone else's property, who will give you property of your own?"

Trusted with a little; trusted with money; trusted with some. one else's stuff—all those things are expressions of integrity, and Daniel obviously had them all. I regularly reminded the inmates that God was watching how they handled their time, the property under their care, and the little money they had. It was common for them to think, "This isn't a big deal, so I will wait until some. thing more important comes along before I really invest myself in doing a good job." That attitude would never allow them to be promoted or trusted and the same is true for you. For some, but I hope not for you, that was a difficult lesson to learn.

If you want to be promoted, it is not enough that you know the Lord. You cannot expect God's favor to open doors for you if you stumble over the threshold because you are ill-equipped for success. You must have the skill and then match it with honesty and faithfulness it you want to reach the highest levels of God's service, no matter what sphere of human existence you are called to serve. I have always laughed at some who talked about God wanting the Church and its members to disciple the nations while those same people could not return a phone call or an email in a timely manner. They talked about excellence; they just didn't know how to produce it.

It was no accident that Daniel rose to the top like cream no matter the circumstances, and your promotion won't be an accident either. It will happen when God knows you are ready, and that involves being "neither negligent nor corrupt." Consider what I say and then commit to a lifestyle that does not look for shortcuts to godly success but pays the price to see it achieved and maintained.

CHAPTER SIXTEEN

CONSPIRACY IN BABYLON

We saw in the last chapter that Daniel did excellent work in Babylon where he was neither "negligent nor corrupt." We learned that God promotes people who have developed their potential and do good work. God's favor, however, does not preclude the jealousy and animosity of others and we will look at that reality in Daniel's life in this chapter.

THE CONSPIRACY

We read that those who could not find fault with Daniel in regard to his work decided to contrive a trap concerning his faith:

> So these administrators and satraps went as a group to the king and said: "May King Darius live forever! The royal administrators, prefects, satraps, advisers and governors have all agreed that the king should issue an edict and enforce the decree that anyone who prays to any god or human being during the next thirty days, except to you, Your Majesty, shall be thrown into the lion's den. Now, Your Majesty, issue the decree and put it in writing so that it cannot be altered in accordance with the law of the Medes and Persians, which cannot be repealed." So King Darius put the decree in writing (Daniel 6:6-9).

Conspiracy and betrayal are not unheard of where the people of God are concerned, especially those who are anointed and chosen by God to lead. We know that Joseph's brothers conspired against him and sold him into slavery in Egypt. David's son Absalom conspired against his father to try and seize the throne. And of course, six hundred years after Daniel, Judas and the Jewish leadership conspired against Jesus to capture, try, and crucify him, thus fulfilling the prediction in Psalm 2:

> Why do the nations conspire and the peoples plot in vain? The kings of the earth rise up and the rulers band together against the Lord and against his anointed, saying, "Let us break their chains and throw off their shackles" (Psalm 2:1-3).

The world and its followers are always trying to undermine or destroy God's people and purpose. When they oppose God's people, they are really opposing God. The opposition we encounter should not surprise us, but it usually does because it can be difficult to fathom how hateful and underhanded people can be.

IMPLICATIONS

I always warned my children not to expect Christian behavior from non-Christians. In fact, I warned them that sometimes we encounter non-Christian behavior from Christians. When 1 taught in a prison setting, 1 urged those listening not to expect people to celebrate their decisions to do the right things. People were watching them and sometimes those people wanted to cause them to stumble (or at least test how serious they were about following the Lord), but they could not base their behavior on what others did or did not do, how they responded or did not respond. They had to learn to do right because it was what God wanted and expected from them.

Let's read what Daniel did when he heard about the king's edict:

> Now when Daniel learned that the decree had been published, he went home to his upstairs room where the windows opened toward Jerusalem. Three times a day he got down on his knees and prayed, giving thanks to his God, just as he had done before. Then these men went as a group and found Daniel praying and asking God for help (Daniel 6:10-11).

Daniel did not back down or compromise. He showed his usual courage by continuing to do what he did for the Lord for all to see. Daniel realized that he needed God's help if he was to survive yet another crisis, so he prayed as he always did. His enemies thought they had him where they wanted him, as we will read in the next Chapter, but Daniel was right where God wanted him and felt safe in his prayer chamber or in the lion's den because he could pray and commune with God in either venue equally well.

How about you? Are you carrying out your purpose and living your values in a public way? Or are you compromising? Are you surprised when others don't celebrate your ethics and perhaps plot against you? Do you put your trust in God to vindicate you? If you are going to thrive in a spiritually-hostile environment, you must learn to expect hostility and animosity. If you can face that and be true to who you claim to be, then the Lord will certainly work on your behalf and eventually, although perhaps not right away sustain you in the midst of your enemies.

CHAPTER SEVENTEEN

LIONS IN BABYLON

In the last chapter, we looked at the conspiracy that took place to remove Daniel from his lofty position in Babylon, probably motivated by the jealousy of those who were less capable than Daniel but yet coveted his position. The only way to get what he had in their mind was to manipulate the king to forbid anyone in the kingdom from praying to any entity but the king. Daniel prayed but was caught in the act, so the king had no choice but to sentence Daniel to the lion's den:

> When the king heard this [that Daniel was praying], he was greatly distressed, he was determined to rescue Daniel and made every effort until sundown to save him. Then the men went as a group to King Darius and said to him, "Remember, Your Majesty, that according to the law of the Medes and Persians no decree or edict that the king issues can be changed." So the king gave the order, and they brought Daniel and threw him into the lion's den. The king said to Daniel, "May your God, whom you serve continually, rescue you!" (Daniel 6:14–16).

The king actually prayed for Daniel's protection, providing us a stunning summary of Daniel's life from the king's perspective, for he said that Daniel was continually serving his God. We all know how the story ends, for God heard the king's prayer and did just that; rescue him.

THREE SLEEPLESS NIGHTS

We are told that the king could not sleep during the night of Daniel's imprisonment: "Then the king returned to his palace and spent the night without eating and without any entertainment being brought to him. And he could not sleep" (Daniel 6:18).

When is the last time that an unbeliever prayed for you or spent a night concerned for your well-being? It's probably been a while, if ever, but that gives you an idea of the impact Daniel made on those around him through his commitment to excellence and his God.

I count three sleepless nights invested in Daniel's dilemma. One was the king's, the other was Daniel's (I assume), and the third was Daniel's protector: "Daniel answered, May the king live forever! My God sent his angel, and he shut the mouths of the lions. They have not hurt me, because I was found innocent in his sight. Nor have I ever done any wrong before you, Your Majesty" (Daniel 6:22-23). Now I know angels don't sleep, and neither does the Lord: "He will not let your foot slip he who watches over you will not slumber; indeed, he who watches over Israel will neither slumber nor sleep" (Psalm 121:3-4). We can rest because God doesn't and is mindful of our situations. The only way you will know that to be true is for God to put you in your own lion's den so He can prove His faithfulness.

TIMES OF TESTING

When I was involved in prison ministry, I prepared the inmates (or tried to do so) for their own lion's den. I warned them that they would be tested and it was not because they had done anything wrong, but because God wanted to reveal to them the truth of His promises of protection, which are many:

- He will cover you with his feathers, and

under his wings you will find refuge; his faithfulness will be your shield and rampart (Psalm 91:4).

- The Lord will keep you from all harm—he will watch over your life; the Lord will watch over your coming and going both now and forevermore (Psalm 121:7-8).

- The Lord protects and preserves them—they are counted among the blessed in the land he does not give them over to the desire of their foes (Psalm 41:2).

- God is our refuge and strength, an ever-present help in trouble (Psalm 46:1).

- You are my hiding place; you will protect me from trouble and surround me with songs of deliverance (Psalm 32:7).

- In peace I will lie down and sleep, for you alone, Lord, make me dwell in safety (Psalm 4:8).

- The Lord is a refuge for the oppressed, a stronghold in times of trouble (Psalm 9:9).

The times of testing provide us with great opportunities to live out the truths found in the verses above. Daniel discovered that truth and so did the king who prayed for his protection.

How about you? Are you in the lion's den? If you are, then you have a wonderful opportunity to apply your faith to the promises above. I trust your den experience is not because of your own irresponsibility but is because of your stand for the Lord and His righteousness in your life. If it is, then stand strong, God has control of the lions and He will shut their mouths: If He does not, it's not because He does not care or cannot do so. It's because He has something better in mind for you. If you are not in the lion's den, then file this away someplace where you can access it, for one day you will be there, and when you are, remember Daniel and God's promises to protect you just like He did him.

CHAPTER EIGHTEEN

REVELATION IN BABYLON

Previously, we saw how God preserved Daniel in the lion's den. Lest anyone think that the lions were passive or uninterested in human visitors, we read, "At the king's command, the men who had falsely accused Daniel were brought in and thrown into the lion's den, along with their wives and children. And before they reached the floor of the den, the lions overpowered them and crushed all their bones" (Daniel 6:24).

God had truly intervened and protected Daniel and, if the book had ended there, we could be satisfied with the many lessons we learned from some fascinating stories in Daniel's life. Yet, we are only at the halfway point of the book when we reach the lion's den.

Daniel was and is considered not only a great administrator and leader but also a prophet. In the midst of the craziness of Babylon and its idolatrous ways, Daniel sought the Lord for wisdom and received insight not only into dreams and administration but also for the Lord's people and purpose in the coming centuries.

NO CEILING

When I spoke in prisons, I would point out to the inmates that they were surrounded by walls, fences, barbed wire, alarm systems, and guards of which they were only too aware. There was little chance for anyone to escape and anyone coming to see them from the outside had to pass through multiple checkpoints. Yet I reminded them that there was no ceiling or roof—nothing between them and the God of heaven. That meant they had free and open access to God through prayer and God in turn could shower them with blessings, wisdom, and revelation concerning His will and ways. I urged them not to wait until they were released to grow and learn to seek the Lord, but rather to do it while they were in—they had an open heaven.

This is important for all of us because we have the tendency to wait until conditions are perfect (or at least better than they are now) before we look to thrive in the things of God. We will take the missions trip when we have more money, go back to school when the kids are done with their education, or pursue purpose when we retire. The key to success and productivity in God is to learn how to make the most of what you have now, using that as your foundation for fruitfulness.

Armed with that truth, I saw many inmates return to school, write books, learn a trade, pray for others, lead small group studies, or preach while they were incarcerated. They were often surprised at how much they could grow and how God could and would use them while they were in their own Babylon and not after they got out. They followed in the steps of Daniel who did the same thing.

REVELATION

God showed unusual things to Daniel in Babylon, There was no way to keep God out of the lion's den, the royal chambers, or Daniel's prayer room. What's more, Daniel kept close records of what he did and saw and received tremendous insight, as we will see in the next few chapters. Daniel suffered in Babylon, but that pain was the foundation for a ministry that has impacted God's people for many centuries since.

Daniel learned the truth of what James, the brother of Jesus, wrote many centuries after Daniel:

> Consider it pure joy, my brothers and sisters, whenever you face trials of many kinds, because you know that the testing of your faith produces perseverance. Let perseverance finish its work so that you may be mature and complete, not lacking anything. If any of you lacks wisdom, you should ask God, Who gives generously to all without finding fault, and it will be given to you. But when you ask, you must believe and not doubt, because the one who doubts is like a wave of the sea, blown and tossed by the wind. That person should not expect to receive anything from the Lord. Such a person is double-minded and unstable in all they do. Believers in humble circumstances ought to take pride in their high position. But the rich should take pride in their humiliation since they will pass away like a wildflower. For the sun rises with scorching heat and withers the plant; its blossom falls and its beauty is destroyed. In the same way, the rich will fade away even while they go about their business. Blessed is the one who perseveres under trial because, having stood the test, that person will receive the crown of life that the Lord has promised to those who love him (James 1:2-12)

Are you waiting for your circumstances to improve until you have more money, more time, more favor with your supervisor, or until you feel better, more inspired, or more motivated—before you step out to do God's will? Can you see that your current circumstances are adequate for you to learn more about the Lord and thrive in His will? If Daniel could receive such insight and understanding in his Babylon, can you have the faith for the same in yours? The writer of Ecclesiastes summed it up when he wrote:

> Whoever watches the wind will not plant;
> whoever looks at the clouds will not reap;
> As you do not know the path of the wind,
> or how the body is formed in a mother's womb, so you cannot understand the
> work of God, the Maker of all things.Sow
> your seed in the morning, and at evening
> let your hands not be idle, for you do not
> know which will succeed, whether this or
> that, or whether both will do equally well
> (Ecclesiastes 11:4-6).

In the next few chapters, we will examine Daniel's specific revelation in Babylon, but for now, let it sink in that your time to shine and be purposeful is not in some future idyllic scenario; it is now. If Daniel did it, you can too for you serve the same God Daniel did, and He will help you, like He did Daniel, be all you can be re gardless of how oppressive or uncomfortable your Babylon is.

CHAPTER NINETEEN

REWARDED IN BABYLON

As we study Daniel's life, we learn that God put Daniel in some difficult situations and never apologized for doing so. We never read of the Lord telling Daniel, David, Jeremiah, Nehemiah, or the Apostle Paul, "Sir, I am so sorry for what I am about to put you through. It is going to be difficult and I considered many others, even interviewed a few, but 1 had no choice but to select you for the suffering and pain ahead of you." No, it is a privilege to serve the Lord in New York City, Beijing, Jerusalem, or Babylon, and God knows what He must put us through to obtain the results He wants.

In this chapter, let's begin to look at the insight Daniel continued to receive in Babylon. Early in the book, he received interpretations to the king's dreams. In the last half of the book, Daniel received special insight into the Lord's plan not only for Babylon but also for the world after Babylon and leading up to the time of Christ. Here are some things to consider as we begin chapter 7:

> In the first year of Belshazzar king of Babylon, Daniel had a dream, and visions passed through his mind as he was lying in bed. He wrote down the substance of his dream…"I, Daniel, was troubled in spirit, and the visions that passed through. my mind disturbed me. I approached one of

those standing there and asked him the meaning of all this. So he told me and gave me the interpretation of these things ..." (Daniel 7:1, 15-16).

THE LESSONS FOR US

Here are some lessons to consider as we move into the second half of Daniel's book:

1. God began to show Daniel things in the first year of Belshazzar, who was the king made famous for the writing on the wall in Daniel 5. Daniel was demoted when this king rose to power, so God had put Daniel on the shelf, so to speak, so he would have time to seek and hear from God. The application for inmates is clear in this instance, but the lesson is the same for all of us. Before we can begin something new, we often have to end something else and wait for the new season to begin. That is seldom easy.

2. Daniel did not trust his memory, but recorded what he saw, which probably occurred at night. We must be ready for God to speak to us and take seriously what He says. Writing it down certainly helps. Do you journal? If not, you have experienced the problem with taking mental notes the ink fades quickly. I urged inmates and I urge you to keep a journal so you can go back and track the progress of your growth and insight into the things of God.

3. Daniel was troubled by what he saw but didn't stop pressing into the Lord.

He sought the Lord for the meaning and Lord was only too ready to fulfill Daniel's request. Knowledge is having the information on a particular subject; wisdom is knowing what to do with the knowledge. God gave Daniel wisdom so he not only knew what the Lord was doing but also what Daniel was to do with what he saw. He knew he was to write it down and publish it.

4. As we read through Daniel 7, we learn that Daniel saw four beasts representing four kingdoms starting with Babylon and leading up to the fourth, most ferocious beast, which symbolized the Roman Empire. Any kingdom or empire that does not serve the Lord becomes a vicious and bloodthirsty beast. There is no hope for man in politics but Daniel did see the hope and breakthrough for mankind.

5. The hope Daniel saw was the "son of man": "In my vision at night I looked, and there before me was one like a *son of man*, coming with the clouds of heaven. He approached the Ancient of Days and was led into his presence. He was given authority, glory and sovereign power, all nations and peoples of every language worshipped him. His dominion is an everlasting dominion that will not pass away; and his kingdom is one that will never be destroyed (Daniel 7:13-14, emphasis added)

DANIEL'S REWARD

What was Daniels reward for what he endured

in Babylon? Daniel, like Abraham, saw the day of the Lord according to Jesus in John 8:56-58. God pulled back the curtains of time and showed Daniel that many powerful kingdoms would arise, similar to the one he was experiencing in Babylon, but God was in control and was going to send one, the "son of man," to strip those kingdoms of their power and authority. It is of note that Jesus' favorite label or name for Himself was the Son of Man, indicating that He (Jesus) was the one who was going to subdue the kingdoms as promised in Daniel's vision.

God did not reveal anything to Daniel about his personal situation or how long he would suffer. God took Daniel to a higher place to see God's purpose in the centuries to come. In a sense, Daniel got a foretaste of what Paul described in Ephesians 2:6-7: "And God raised us up with Christ and seated us with him in the heavenly realms in Christ Jesus, in order that in the coming ages he might show the incomparable riches of his grace, expressed in his kindness to us in Christ Jesus."

I urged prisoners to use their time behind bars to seek the Lord, not for their own comfort or relief, or for insight into their limited world, but to seek Him for the purpose of God beyond them so they could pray, teach, and write about God's plan in the earth, not only the one in their prison. One discipleship group I led actually write a book *The 7 Habits of Highly Effective Inmates*. They were truly Daniel's brothers following his example, and they succeeded in their Babylon as Daniel did in his.

Now it's your turn not just to survive in your health, economic, career, ministry, prison, or relational Babylon but also to thrive there. That will only happen when you move beyond the self-centered, limited boundaries of your own world to the limitless expanse of God's purpose for His world. Are you up to the task? I hope you are, but remember, your reward is not personal comfort but God's presence in sumptuous portions.

CHAPTER TWENTY

MYSTERIES IN BABYLON

We have learned that through all Daniel encountered in Babylon, he stayed true to the Lord and served his God. Tradition has it that when the first of those in Babylonian exile returned to Judea, Daniel refused to accompany them, preferring to spend his last days in the land far away from home where God had chosen to send him.

Not only did the Lord show Daniel the spiritual reality of his. own day, but also revealed to him things that were in the future and yet to come. In a sense, Daniel was the first of the end-time prophets, which is remarkable considering where he was (Babylon) and what he was doing (a government official). Yet Daniel was the precursor to a worldwide movement that transitioned God's people from the comforts of their homeland in Israel to a strategy that reached the whole world with God's message of love and forgiveness. Daniel was a pioneer of sorts and proved that God's purpose and revelation are not dependent upon geography (where one is) but rather on purpose (what God has assigned one to do).

IT'S A MYSTERY

Daniel was overwhelmed with what he saw about God's purposes for the Earth:

> Then the sovereignty, power and greatness of all the kingdoms under heaven

will be handed over to the holy people of the Most High. His kingdom will be an everlasting kingdom, and all rulers will worship and obey him "This is the end of the matter. I, Daniel, was deeply troubled by my thoughts, and my face turned pale, but I kept the matter to myself" (Daniel 7:27-28).

On another occasion, Daniel tried to make sense of what he was seeing, but concluded,

"The vision of the evenings and mornings that has been given you is true, but seal up the vision, for it concerns the distant future." I, Daniel, was worn out. I lay exhausted for several days. Then I got up and went about the king's business. I was appalled by the vision; it was beyond understanding (Daniel 8:26-27).

When I was involved in prison ministry, I urged the inmates to use the time they had to seek the Lord and learn more about His ways. They were in their own Babylon, but God wanted to reveal Himself to them in more ways than helping them understand their own personal situation or get them back home to their world. God wanted to show them His purpose beyond prison, for them and for others. I worked with one discipleship group that wrote a book titled *The 7 Habits of Highly Effective Inmates*, which was distributed to other prisons beyond the one where it was written. That was exactly what I was trying to teach them— that God had something more in mind for them than serving their time and making them comfortable. The same is true for you.

BEYOND UNDERSTANDING

Perhaps you are in a tough place and you are

seeking God for the meaning of it all. God is not obligated to explain it all to you and you would be wise to conclude as Daniel did that "it is beyond understanding." That is how suffering is. It doesn't make sense except that you live in a fallen world and that somehow God uses your pain for your good. Suffering plays a role in your personal development and those who succeed in breaking out of their world of pain to minister to others in pain (like Daniel did) are the most successful—as God defines success. Peter wrote about suffering and you would do well to heed his words:

> Therefore, since Christ suffered in his body, arm yourselves also with the same attitude, because whoever suffers in the body is done with sin. As a result, they do not live the rest of their earthly lives for evil human desires, but rather for the will of God. For you have spent enough time in the past doing what pagans choose to do living in debauchery, lust, drunkenness, orgies, carousing and detestable idolatry (1 Peter 4:1-3),

and

> Dear friends, do not be surprised at the fiery ordeal that has come on you to test you, as though something strange were happening to you. But rejoice inasmuch as you participate in the sufferings of Christ, so that you may be overjoyed when his glory is revealed. If you are insulted because of the name of Christ, you are blessed, for the Spirit of glory and of God rests on you. If you suffer, it should not be as a murderer or thief or any other kind of criminal, or even as a meddler How. ever, if you suffer as a Christian, do not be ashamed,

but praise God that you bear that name (1 Peter 4:12-16).

Are you suffering? Are you trying to make sense of it when there is no sense to be made? Then it's time to change your tactics. Try using your situation to learn more about Him and then share what you learn with others. Daniel did the one thing he could do with what he saw: He recorded it.

Today, we read it and are blessed because he did not give in to self-pity and refused to be consumed by the pain. That would be a good strategy for you as well. Don't let your Babylon be your prison, but let it be the launching pad for missiles of prayer and testimonies that speak of God's goodness even when you don't understand what in the world He is doing or why.

CHAPTER TWENTY-ONE

ESTEEMED IN BABYLON

It's time to move on to chapter nine where we read that Daniel is once again seeking the Lord:

> "Now, our God, hear the prayers and petitions of your servant. For your sake, Lord, look with favor on your desolate sanctuary. Give ear, our God, and hear; open your eyes and see the desolation of the city that bears your Name. We do not make requests of you because we are righteous, but because of your great mercy. Lord, listen! Lord, forgive! Lord, hear and act! For your sake, my God, do not delay, because your city and your people bear your Name" (Daniel 9:17-19).

Like Nehemiah after him, Daniel spent a great deal of time as described in chapter nine crying out to God on behalf of his people. He enumerated and repented of his people's sins, and called on the Lord to have mercy.

One of the things I would point out to the inmates when I was involved in prison ministry was the sheer amount of time they had on their hands and the chance to use it for good: study, service, prayer, and personal development. You may not have as much time as inmates who are serving "time," but you still have 24 hours a day. What are you doing with your time? I am currently revamping my daily routine because I am not happy with my level of productivity and development. I must use the time I have effectively. Daniel certainly did and used the time he had to touch and reach heaven and make a different on Earth.

GOD IS WATCHING

After Daniel's prayer, he had another angelic visitation to teach and inform him:

> While I was speaking and praying, confessing my sin and the sin of my people Israel and making my request to the Lord my God for his holy hill—while I was still in prayer, Gabriel, the man I had seen in the earlier vision, came to me in swift flight about the time of the evening sacrifice. He instructed me and said to me, "Daniel, I have now come to give you insight and understanding. As soon as you began to pray, a word went out, which I have come to tell you, for you are highly esteemed. Therefore, consider the word and understand the vision" (Daniel 9:20-23, emphasis added).

The phrase I want you to see if that Daniel was highly esteemed. Can you imagine? Heaven knew who Daniel was and it seems that he had a special place in the heart of God and the beings of heaven. God heard what Daniel prayed. God was moved by Daniel's selfless service and exceptional attitude. God was watching Daniel and God is watching you. Are you doing things to distinguish yourself to God? Or do you expect God to do what you want when you want it just because, well, just because you are who you are and that's what you want?

This makes me think of another man whom God honored and esteemed for his exceptional service in God's kingdom, and that man is the Apostle Paul. When Paul was on the ship heading to Rome and a major storm made it look like all was lost, Luke wrote this report of Paul's words:

> "Last night an angel of the God to whom i belong and whom I serve stood beside me and said, 'Do not be afraid, Paul. You must stand trial before Caesar; and God has graciously given you the lives of all who sail with you! So keep up your courage, men, for I have faith in God that it will happen just as he told me" (Acts 27:23-25, emphasis added).

Because Paul was on the ship and God recognized his service, all the other passengers were spared. Is your presence with others that important and powerful? Does God protect them because of you? I encouraged the inmates to take this truth seriously and not wait until they were released to make an impact for the Lord (and some were never getting out). Daniel was highly esteemed as an exile in Babylon; inmates can be highly favored in prison; and you can garner God's attention as you serve Him in your difficult life situation.

Are you trying to escape where you are, or are you serving the Lord and others from that place? Have you surrendered the control of your life to Him, deciding to be content where you are? Are you holding God's purpose for you hostage until He meets your demands and only then will you release your gifts to serve Him? I urge you to do what you can to earn heaven's favor now, right where you are with what you have. Pray, repent, confess, declare, seek, and devote your life to His purpose for you, and I promise you will capture the attention of heaven, and when heaven is pleased with you, who can be against you?

CHAPTER TWENTY-TWO

POWER IN BABYLON

In the last chapter, I alluded to the Apostle Paul when he was a prisoner on a ship heading to Rome. The ship ran aground but before it did, an angel appeared to Paul and foretold what would happen. The angel assured Paul that no lives would be lost, after which he told the crew, "So keep up your courage, men, for I have faith in God that it will happen just as he told me. Nevertheless, we must run aground on some island" (Acts 27:26-27). Now my question to you is this: Who was in charge—who had the power—on that ship? Was it the experienced sailors? No, it was Paul, for he was the only one who had clarity as to what was going on.

That leads us to this next-to-last lesson about Daniel and his exile in Babylon, and I will ask the same question as above: Who was really the leader in Babylon? Was it the king? Was it his wise men and advisors? Was it the armed guards or army that surrounded and protected the king? No, I would insist it was Daniel, and let me devote the rest of this chapter to explain why I make that claim.

THE REAL POWER

Daniel was the real leader for six reasons. Since Daniel's purpose was to be a source and dispenser of wisdom in Babylon, I will use the book of Proverbs (all verses from the NKJV) to justify mw claim that the true leadership power resided in and with God's prophet and administrator:

1. The power of wisdom: A wise man is strong yes, a man of knowledge increases strength (Proverbs 24:5).

2. The power of revelation: Counsel is mine, and sound wisdoms I am understanding, I have strength (Proverbs 8:14).

3. The power of service: Whoever keeps the fig tree will eat its fruit; so he who waits on his master will be honored (Proverbs 27:18).

4. The power of excellence: Do you see a man who excels in his work? He will stand before kings; he will not stand before unknown men (Proverbs 22:29).

5. The power of prayer. The sacrifice of the wicked is an abomination to the Lord, but the prayer of the upright is His delight (Proverbs 15:8).

6. The power of integrity: The integrity of the upright will guide them, but the perversity of the unfaithful will destroy them (Proverbs 10:9).

Daniel was a man of power, and his life was undergirded by his spiritual disciplines and commitment to do exceptional work as he fulfilled his purpose. God promoted him not based on potential but on the fact that Daniel developed his potential. Daniel served four separate kings in three different kingdoms, withstanding change and the whims of kings to ascend to the heights of governmental service where God had planted him.

This was an important lesson for inmates during my prison ministry days for obvious reasons. They were walled in and surrounded by armed guards. Many felt they had to be out of their Babylon before they could serve God and be effective. Our team taught them that they could be powerful and lead where they were. The same is true for you. Are you in prison in more ways than one? Are you hemmed in by your circumstances and also by how you view your circumstances? If you see them as limiting, then you will be limited. If you see them as irrelevant or as the means by which God is preparing you for greatness, then you will lead, regardless of your title.

CAN YOU DO ALL THINGS?

There is a verse at the end of Daniel that summarizes his life and it is found in Daniel 11:32: "Those who do wickedly against the covenant he shall corrupt with flattery; but the people who know their God shall be strong, and carry out great exploits." There is no doubt that Daniel did great exploits in his day; can the same be said for you in your day? If you quote Philippians 4:13, "I can do all things through Christ who strengthens me," then let me ask you one final question: Can you describe what the "all things" are that you are doing? The word can is a statement of potential but not necessarily the fulfillment of that potential. Daniel lived in his potential and he serves as a model for us, whether incarcerated or not, to follow so we can bear the fruit God wants us to bear.

In the next chapter, we will look at one aspect of the Christmas story as it relates to Daniel, for his influence extended five hundred years after he lived. As we come to a close, I pray that you will accept the fact that you have power to lead not based on authority or title only but based on the fact that you know your God, and that gives you strength to carry out great exploits for Him.

CHAPTER TWENTY-THREE

DANIEL AND
THE WISE MEN

There are many fascinating aspects of the Christmas story, not the least of which is the Magi who showed up to welcome the new king who had been born. We read in Matthew,

> After Jesus was born in Bethlehem in Judea, during the time of King Herod, Magi from the east came to Jerusalem and asked, "Where is the one who has been born king of the Jews?
>
> We saw his star when it rose and have come to worship him." When King Herod heard this he was disturbed, and all Jerusalem with him. When he had called together all the people's chief priests and teachers of the law, he asked them where the Messiah was to be born ... After they had heard the king, they went on their way, and the star they had seen when it rose went ahead of them until it stopped over the place where the child was. When they saw the star, they were overjoyed. On coming to the house, they saw the child with his mother Mary, and they bowed down and worshipped him. Then they opened their treasures and presented him with gifts of gold, frankincense and myrrh. And having been warned

in a dream not to go back to Herod, they returned to their country by another route (Matthew 2:1-4, 9-12).

Who were these Magi? What were they looking for when they saw and followed the star? To answer those questions, let's learn a little more about these mystery men.

THE MAGI

Dr. Craig Chester, past president of the Monterey Institute for Research in Astronomy, gave the following description of the Magi (retrieved from http://tifwe.org/wcontent/uploads/2011/12/The-Star-of-Bethlehem.pdf):

> Magi is the plural of Magus, the root of our word magic, and "court astrologers" is probably the best translation, although "wise men" is also a good term, descriptive of the esteem in which they were widely held. The group of Magi in question came "from the East." They might have been Zoroastrians, Medes, Persians, Arabs, or even Jews. They probably served as court advisors, making forecasts and predictions for their royal patrons based on their study of the stars, about which they were quite knowledgeable. Magi often wandered from court to court, and it was not unusual for them to cover great distances in order to attend the birth or crowning of a king, paying their respects and offering gifts. It is not surprising, therefore, that Matthew would mention them as validation of Jesus' kingship, or that Herod would regard their arrival as a very serious matter.

He adds, "The Magi were such important

significant individuals they would rot have traveled alone. In fact, they probably traveled with a very large entourage including soldiers, even a small army for protection. So it should not be surprising that Herod and the citizens of Jerusalem were troubled when they arrived."

But how did these Magi know what to look for in the sky and, when they found it, then decide to make the long trek to Judea to welcome the new king? The answer is where Daniel enters into the story.

DANIEL'S INFLUENCE

There were marry jews in Babylon who did not return after their exile was over. One of them was Daniel who we know was appointed "chief of the magicians, enchanters, astrologers and diners' (Daniel 5:11), There is no doubt that Daniel's peers and his fellow Jewish exiles would have been familiar with Daniel's prophetic insight into the kingdoms that were to follow Babylon. These Magi heard something from Daniel that intrigued them to such an extent that they studied the heavens and Daniel's writ Ings for 500 years until one day when a star appeared. They were, convinced that they had found what they were looking for and what Daniel had predicted. They decided to make the long journey, probably with an entourage of soldiers and personal aides, to welcome the new king. No wonder Herod and all Jerusalem were disturbed when the Magi appeared,

As we close this book, we see that Daniel's purpose in going to Babylon far exceeded his own awareness, God had a plan for his life that transcended his generation. I would encourage inmates with the same truth that God has a plan for their lives, even though they were incarcerated in a place not of their choosing. Daniel was faithful to his prison sentence to continue serving the lord and God used him mightily. The same was and is true for the inmates, and it is true for you.

Whenever we celebrate the birth of Jesus, let's recommit ourselves to live a life of purpose and creativity, not ones our circumstances improve but right now right where we are. Daniel serve, wrote, spoke, advised, and prayed in Babylon. As I have mentioned earlier, he may have been imprisoned behind walls but there was no roof. He had direct access to heaven and heaven could reach and touch him. No Babylonian leader or wise man could prevent that. You can succeed in your Babylon if you are determined to find the Lord there and not try to escape. Who knows what God can and will do through you if you stop focusing on the "out there" and start focusing on the here and now.

ABOUT THE AUTHOR

John founded a personal and leadership development company, called *PurposeQuest*, in 2001 and today travels the world to speak, consult and inspire leaders and people everywhere. From 2001-2008, he spent six months a year in Africa and still enjoys visiting and working on that continent. Most recently, John founded Urban Press, a publishing service designed to tell stories of the city, from the city and to the city. John is the author of more than 75 books.

KEEP IN
TOUCH WITH
JOHN W. STANKO

www.purposequest.com
www.johnstanko.us
www.stankobiblestudy.com
www.stankomondaymemo.com
or via email at johnstanko@gmail.com

John also does extensive relief and community development work in Kenya. You can see some of his projects at

www.purposequest.com/contributions

PurposeQuest International
PO Box 8882
Pittsburgh, PA 15221-0882

ADDITIONAL TITLES BY JOHN STANKO

Live the Word Commentary: Matthew
Live the Word Commentary: Mark
Live the Word Commentary: Luke
Live the Word Commentary: John
Live the Word Commentary: Acts
Live the Word Commentary: Romans
Live the Word Commentary: 1 & 2 Corinthians
Live the Word Commentary: Galatians, Ephesians, Philippians, Colossians, Philemon
Live the Word Commentary: 1 & 2 Thessalonians, 1 & 2 Timothy, and Titus
Live the Word Commentary: Hebrews
Live the Word Commentary: Revelation

Ediciones en Español

Cambiando la Manera de Hacer Iglesia

La Vida Es Una Mina De Oro:
Te Atreves A Cavarla?

No Leas Estes Libro: (A Menos Que Quieras
Convertirte E Un Mejor Líder)

Fuero lo Viejo, Adentro lo Nuevo

Gemas de Propósito

Ven a Adorarlo: Preparándonos para Emmanuel